THE WINNER
NAMES THE AGE

Edited by Michelle Cliff

Preface by Paula Snelling

––––––––––

W · W · NORTON & COMPANY · INC · NEW YORK

THE WINNER NAMES THE AGE

A COLLECTION OF WRITINGS BY LILLIAN SMITH

Copyright © 1978 by W. W. Norton & Company, Inc.
Published simultaneously in Canada by George J. McLeod Limited,
Toronto. Printed in the United States of America.
All Rights Reserved
First Edition

Book Design by Antonina Krass
Display type is typositor Andrich Minerva
Text type is V.I.P. Electra
Manufactured by Vail-Ballou Press, Inc.

Library of Congress Cataloging in Publication Data

Smith, Lillian Eugenia, 1897–1966.
The winner names the age.

I. Cliff, Michelle.   II. Title.
PS3537.M653W5   1978   814'.5'2   78-7222
ISBN 0-393-08826-X

1 2 3 4 5 6 7 8 9 0

Teach us to listen to sounds larger than our own heartbeat;
that endure longer than our own weeping in the dark.

—LILLIAN SMITH

Contents

9

III OF WOMEN, MEN, AND AUTOBIOGRAPHY

PREFACE

Lillian Smith was born female, white, southern, at the threshold of the twentieth century. This convergence of gender, color, place, and time afforded her vantage (some might say disadvantage) points shared by few writers. Each contributed, in obvious or subtle ways, to her stature as artist and human being. The sights, sounds, smells, the cadences of speech, body language, rituals and rotes of her region entered her bloodstream in childhood, and give sensory verisimilitude to her writings. She did not sever this taproot, although her early, hometown search for the *whys* became a worldwide and lifelong quest.

The universality of her writings comes, not in spite of their locale, but more *because* her South was (and she saw it so) both dramatic stageset and potential proving ground for success or failure in the inevitable confrontations of races and cultures. She knew that the continents, with their various spiritual and material poverty and wealth, were no longer moated by oceans; she recognized that we are inhabitants of a small world whose common humanity demands humility, mutual appreciation of cultural and individual diversities, and the cross-fertilization of the ideas of all peoples.

The contribution her life and art made toward this end was, I

11

believe, enhanced rather than diminished by the fact that she was a woman living in a man-made society. She was, of course, intimately aware of the barriers (some surmountable, some not) placed in the path of any woman of her time and place seeking wholeness and success in professional, personal, and artistic life. She aided those individuals and groups who worked for improvements in women's rights, just as she made organizational and other efforts to attain black rights. Her personal bent and qualifications fitted her best, however, for seeking fuller identification of, and with *human* needs and envisionment of humane ways of filling them. She knew the sharp two-edgedness of swords that separate; she had seen that men no less than women, whites no less than blacks, are deformed and stunted by arbitrary exclusions of the other from full human status.

Lillian Smith was born on December 12, 1897, in Jasper, Florida, into a large, comfortably affluent family who were leaders in community, church, and financial affairs. When she was in her mid-teens her father's business (naval stores) failed due to wartime shipping disruptions. The family moved from Florida to Georgia, into what had been their summer mountain home. The warmth of these childhood years, along with a few minor bewilderments, are caught in her *Memory of a Large Christmas*. Chapters in *Killers of the Dream* and *The Journey* go deeper into the dark and the light etchings made on the sensitive spirit of a child confronted with the anomalies of the civilization and circumstances in which these early years were lived. The Maxwell, Georgia, of her novel *Strange Fruit*, so far as it had specific geographical location and cultural milieu, was the town she left at age seventeen and to which she never returned.

Lillian Smith was on her own financially from 1915 to the end of her life. After working her way through a year of college and three years at the Peabody Conservatory of Music in Baltimore, she went to China for three years, which she spent as head of music at a Methodist school in Huchow. Two decades later, she commented on those years:

The turmoil within me; I was now questioning many aspects of our Western life; my keen new interest in world affairs, in psychiatry, in India, Gandhi . . . all of these stimuli kept me keyed high so that I become aware of many many things about the human condition. But what I loved were the canals, the walled cities, the sampans, the *walla-walla* of the street people, the little shops; the temples at the top of the mountains, the stone steps you climbed to get there, the pilgrims you met along the way, tea with the priest at the top. Suddenly, I wanted to write about it. And I did, later: about a handful of white women and a school of Chinese girls, the relationships, the loneliness, the passions, the self-imposed disciplines . . . all these against the vast future changes that even then were straining at all of China.

This novel, written in the thirties, was rejected by the publishers to whom it was sent as too "shocking" and "revolutionary." It was burned, later, in the fire which destroyed her home, other manuscripts, and some ten thousand letters of irreplaceable human and historical value.

In 1925 Lillian Smith's father, in failing health, asked her to return home and take over the camp for girls which he had started in 1920. She acceded, as an act of love-duty, though without illusions as to the cost to her personal life and her career in music. As director, she made Laurel Falls Camp into a place of such creativity and growth that few who summered there over the next twenty-three years do not still treasure those months as among the most joyous and enriching of their lives.

During those periods when she was not occupied with the camp, she began and continued the career for which she is most widely known. In the first decade she wrote her China novel and three other manuscripts. (These last were not published, being too identifiably based on living, vulnerable people; they too were burned in the fire of 1955.) Her first appearance in print came in the little magazine which she started in 1936 and terminated in 1945. The magazine grew—from 12 pages and 27 subscribers to 110 pages and 10,000 subscribers—and became an important stimulus for both blacks and whites as they confronted and questioned the status quo of their region.*

Lillian Smith's first published novel was *Strange Fruit* (1944), heralded at first as "powerful," written by an "astonishingly talented" author. Then, suddenly, a furor broke. No longer was the literary or human value of the book important. Now it was called "obscene" and attacked (or defended) in headlines, editorials, columns, and the Massachusetts courts for months; its author becoming one of the most "controversial" figures in American letters. Lillian Smith's offense was imputed to be the one-time use of one four-letter word (more profusely and less discreetly used in many a noncontroversial book of the same decade). It will be obvious to most readers that her "sin" lay not in any conventional obscenity but in the blasphemy of breaking the conspiracy of silence behind which her region had maintained (and sold) its illusion of solidarity; and in telling the story of a love relationship between a black woman and a white man in the Deep South with such compassionate clarity that the deadend-edness of skin worship, for adherents anywhere, would now be evident to readers everywhere.

The next two published works were nonfiction: *Killers of the Dream* (1949; revised 1962) and *The Journey* (1954). In the first she told about that part of her life which had been shared by most white southerners: how we were taught to act, feel, and become White. In *The Journey* she shared the epiphanies which were hers as she sought to find and define the meaning of life. These two were followed by a novel, *One Hour* (1959), a spiritual whodunit of the fifties, that decade in which suspicion, seduction, ignorance, and fear peaked, wrecking so many lives—including those of her three protagonists, a dancer, scientist, and priest, whose affections and fates were intermeshed. There were three other books, shorter and more topical, but of continuing worth: *Now Is the Time* (1955), a cogent plea to her region to cease its defiance of the Supreme Court decision; the evoc-

* An anthology, *From the Mountain*, of writings from *South Today* was published in 1972 by Memphis State University Press, edited by Helen White and Redding S. Sugg, Jr.

ative *Memory of a Large Christmas* (1961); and *Our Faces, Our Words* (1964), a depiction of the shared exhilarations and disappointments, and some private inner conflicts, of young blacks and whites working together in the civil rights movement.

Lillian Smith died on September 28, 1966, after a thirteen-year battle with cancer. She is buried on the mountain where she lived and which she loved. Her last paragraph in *The Journey* reveals the resonances of her life better than another's words can:

> To believe in something not yet proved and to underwrite it with our lives: it is the only way we can leave the future open. Man, surrounded by facts, permitting himself no surmise, no intuitive flash, no great hypothesis, no risk is in a locked cell. Ignorance cannot seal the mind and imagination more surely. To find the point where hypothesis and fact meet; the delicate equilibrium between dream and reality; the place where fantasy and earthy things are metamorphosed into a work of art; the hour when faith in the future becomes knowledge of the past; to lay down one's power for others in need; to shake off the old ordeal and get ready for the new; to question, knowing that never can the full answer be found; to accept uncertainties quietly, even our incomplete knowledge of God: this is what man's journey is about, I think.

Her last interviewer said of Lillian Smith, "She went on writing and speaking, driven to that most outrageous and bewildering of human acts, which is saying the simple, obvious truth before people are ready to hear it." Overall, that is an accurate appraisal, but I want to add something with regard to all her writings, and specifically to the speeches and essays presented here. Though they lived in communities indifferent or hostile to these ideas, the smaller groups who were her audiences were hungering to hear such words said aloud. Had they not been spoken by someone, in such manner as she said them, and at such times and places as they were said, the acceleration of change that has occurred in the last quarter-century could not have taken place.

In the altered climate now existing, larger audiences will find interest and value in reading these pages. They will see Lillian Smith as a vibrant participant in her present, addressing the urgent crises of those decades. They will also find that she was a keen student of her past, and a dreamer always of the quality of the future which human beings can yet make for themselves and their children. She knew the eternal oneness of the tenses.

Paula Snelling
November 1977

A NOTE ON THE TEXT

The essays and speeches in this book—because they span a wide expanse of history and subject—are divided into three parts which are introduced by headnotes. Most of these writings are reprinted in their entirety. In a few cases elisions have been made; these are clearly marked by asterisks, and were required to avoid repetition, thus making the writings herein into a coherent whole. Changes in wording are also clearly marked, and have been made only on the grounds of clarity. This has been necessary in most cases where the selection, given as a speech, was not thereafter prepared by the author for appearance in print. (Some speeches previously appeared in full or in part in magazines such as the *New Republic*, *New Leader*, *Progressive*, *Phylon*, and *Saturday Review*.)

I

ADDRESSED
TO THE SOUTH

Part I of this collection consists of writings which speak directly to the citizens of the South and contain Lillian Smith's specific suggestions for political and social change, along with her philosophical analysis of why such change is necessary. The selections are arranged chronologically and are a historical record of segregation and the opposition to segregation in the South, from 1942–1966, the date of Lillian Smith's last speech.

The politicians named in this part, and throughout the book, were mentioned by Lillian Smith simply because they were being publicized in the media at the time she was speaking, and their then-current words were familiar to the audiences she was addressing. Some of these men are now dead, others are no longer in public life. Those in the public eye today do not use such language. Some have probably changed their minds and hearts; if not, they use carefully chosen code-words to get their messages across to today's listeners. The journalists whose names appear here, except the then-syndicated columnist Westbrook Pegler, were among the more liberal of their day, and Lillian Smith was calling attention only to unfortunate lapses on their part, from their customarily higher standards.

The first selection in Part I, "Are We Not All Confused," an editorial from *South Today* (1942), responds to a question posed by a young black woman: "I am confused. To whom do I owe my loyalty? to my own people? to white America? to the darker races?" Her question describes the black situation in World War II: How it was demanded that blacks, in the midst of a burgeoning struggle to become complete and total citizens, put aside their struggle for the "larger" one of defending "their" country both at home and abroad. Smith addresses the hypocrisy of those who speak in favor of black rights during periods of peace and during wartime accuse blacks of treason: "who seem to feel that attempts to increase racial democracy while fighting a war for democracy are not only irrelevant but dangerously inciting . . ." In this essay, as in her other writing, Lillian Smith patiently lists ways in which racism can be gradually and nonviolently overthrown, emphasizing that segregation is the political policy of the few wielded over the essentially uncommitted many.

"Children and Color," two brief statements excerpted from speeches given in 1943 and 1944, express one of Lillian Smith's central concerns: that all children—black and white—are profoundly affected by the restrictions of segregation; that the evil of segregation derives from the limits it places on human possibility for growth in all areas and for all people.

"Humans in Bondage," an essay from *Social Action* (1944), is a compendium of Smith's philosophy regarding racism and a list of practical methods for change. She repeats her concern in "Children and Color," that segregation limits both blacks and whites. She again observes that segregation is perpetuated not by majority rule but by the tacit support given demagogues by otherwise sane and decent people. She expresses here, as elsewhere, her belief in the ability of southern whites to change once they realize the human cost of segregation. There is, she states, no "Negro problem":

> There is a problem facing each of us, black and white, but it is not the "Negro problem." It is the problem, for Negroes, of finding some way to live with white people. It is the problem, for whites, of learning to live with themselves.

Smith—who wrote this essay for a church publication—addresses the churches of the South and the churchgoers, acknowledging the potential power of these organizations to direct change based on the principles they claim to follow.

"Ten Years from Today," a commencement address given at Kentucky State College (1951), is a speech in which Lillian Smith expresses great hope in the beginnings of change in the South. She lists those changes which have already taken place: blacks in southern white institutions of higher education; blacks on city councils in the South; the upsurge in black voting. She observes that the price of these changes has not been cheap—that beatings and deaths have taken place—but that these changes represent a crack in the barrier of segregation which now must, with constant effort, begin to crumble. Perhaps the greatest change, as she sees it, is what she calls "the breaking of the old conspiracy of silence"—the breaking of the tacit support of demagoguery.

In "The Right Way Is Not a Moderate Way," a speech sponsored by the Montgomery Improvement Association and read at the Institute for Non-Violence and Social Change on the date of the first anniversary of the Montgomery bus boycott (December 5, 1956), Lillian Smith endorses nonviolent extremism as the only way to bring about radical change in society. She points out that "moderation," a word of great currency in the 1950s, accomplishes nothing except the maintenance of the status quo. In this speech, which she was unable to deliver in person due to her recurring struggle with cancer, Smith uses the powerful and courageous metaphor of segregation as cancer; a cancer which will metastasize unless extreme rather than moderate measures are taken.

"No Easy Way—Now," a speech given for the Arkansas Council on Human Welfare at the University of Arkansas on October 28, 1957, following the crisis at Little Rock, contains Lillian Smith's delineation of the mob as a threefold phenomenon: there is the obvious mob, represented by the brutality of the Klan; the "quiet well-bred mob" which inhabits "air-conditioned offices" on Main Street, and whose *real power* protects and supports mob number one; and, finally, there is the mob in men's minds, which permits the existence of the first two. To explain mob number three Lillian Smith introduces concepts which she develops in other speeches and articles. These include: the mythic mind, the human ability to symbolize, the dehumanization of man.

"The Moral and Political Significance of the Students' Non-Violent Protests," delivered by Lillian Smith at the All Souls Unitarian Church in Washington, D.C., on April 21, 1960, takes as its point of departure the lunch-counter sit-in by four young blacks in Greensboro, North Carolina. She urges support for the protests of these young people and again affirms the ability of southerners to change. Contrary to its stereotype, the South is not a monolith; it is made up of individuals of "gradations of opinion" and "gradations of moral strength."

Lillian Smith's acceptance speech for the Charles S. Johnson award—her final speech—concludes this section. It is a speech which expresses enormous faith in human possibilities: "as we search for means of collaborating *as human beings for human ends*. This search is the big job of our age; a purpose we should commit ourselves to, whether we are artists or scientists or technicians or teachers or religious leaders. As one writer I have tried, only to work toward this end."

ARE WE NOT ALL CONFUSED?*

A young Negro girl spoke at a recent gathering: "I am confused," she said. "To whom do I owe my loyalty? to my own
people? to white America? to the darker races?"

A Tennessee paper laughed and called it the year's silliest question. (The Queen of France once laughed and made an immortal
wisecrack and France paid for her laughter and that wisecrack, for
the blindness of those in power, and is paying today for the same
kind of blindness.)

There are thirteen million Negroes in this country, not one of
whom has his full Constitutional rights as a citizen. In some regions
in certain cities, he is permitted many of these rights. In others he
has few of them; in most rural regions he has none. In the South, the
Negro loses out on all counts: education, health, recreation, housing, the vote, jobs both as to pay and kind, civil liberties, right of free
movement, right to the courtesies of address which civilized countries accord citizens regardless of race and economic status.

* Editorial, *South Today*, Spring 1942.

Old facts . . . familiar to white minds, unknown to white feelings, are now lashing Negro minds and feelings into deeper confusion.

There is grave need for the white man and the black man in the South to understand each other. It is a necessity today for the intelligent white to use all the imagination he can lay hold of in an attempt to put himself in the Negro's place and learn *how it feels* to be there. It is as much a necessity for the intelligent Negro to try to understand the cultural and psychic factors which cripple the best of white southerners.

For patterns of discrimination and segregation to which the white man is so accustomed that he deems it his American "right" to impose them at pleasure upon the Negro, take on razor edge now as they are carried into the war effort.

For eighty years, in legal freedom, the American Negro has endured these patterns. Not as slave but as American citizen he now asks this question: *when will the patterns be changed?* He believes that the government which requires him to pay taxes and conscripts his sons to fight its war owes him democracy's privileges as well as its duties. He believes quite simply that as a citizen he has an inalienable right to protest the nationwide denial of his Constitutional freedoms. He believes that except for the vote (which he does not have in the South) the right to protest is the only peaceful method of free peoples to correct the wrongs done them. It is a method in good repute among democracies. It is the American way of helping citizens in trouble. The Negro press is now using this way to tell the country of Negro needs. Through its press, the Negro race is asking for the freedoms the United States says it believes in. And the race has been answered that the time is not "right."

When will the time be "right"? and "right" for whom?

The Negro wants to know.

These are questions which bore deep into the core of American democracy. They are questions to be answered; not questions to be dismissed by hush-hush campaigns, or avoided by talks on morale, or settled by white men calling in Negro leaders, closing doors, and laying upon Negro shoulders the heavy burden of responsibility for averting "race trouble."

Nor are they answered by the loud accusations of Westbrook Pegler, or the more restrained but as unfair rebukes of Virginius Dabney
and John Temple Graves (both of whom in peace time made honor-
able efforts in defense of the Negro)—who seem to feel that attempts
to increase racial democracy while fighting a war for democracy are
not only irrelevant but dangerously inciting; who accuse the Negro
press of exploiting the war emergency to stir up race issues, of being
(in Pegler's words) "reminiscent of Hearst at his worst in their sensa-
tionalism and their obvious inflammatory bias."

It is a confused situation in which intelligent men who have
shown their good will by past actions are now behaving as if driven
by stupidity. (One makes no defense of Mr. Pegler. His words too
often betray perverse resistance to change and incomprehension of
human needs for one to believe in either his good will or his intelligence.) But there is need to explain, if one can, the actions of
Mr. Dabney and Mr. Graves—not only because of friendly feelings
for them and admiration for their past achievements, but because
they stand as symbol of all southern liberals. They are of the "best element" in southern culture; of the group whose strengths have
helped build a better South in peacetime but whose weaknesses may
now be its (and the country's) undoing. No one can question these
liberals' integrity or good intentions. Then why, in time of need,
have they failed so completely to understand the Negro's position?
How can they fail to see that were they black they would surely protest their humiliations, that their manhood would cry out in loud
shame against the discriminations imposed upon them?

It is not easy to understand the white southern liberal (and his
northern brother) torn as he is by cultural ambivalences. But let us
try:

Under stress men tend to revert to early patterns of behavior.
Those who are observant recognize this in the regressive habits of
childhood: thumb-sucking, bed-wetting, baby talk, crying, tan-
trums, upon which children fall back so easily when hard pressed by
reality. In adult psychic disturbances, one sees regressions more
severe and more "shocking" but of a similar nature. Whether one is
mentally ill or healthy, one's behavior under stress is trued to the

same basic principles. White southerners are rigorously trained in childhood to believe in their whiteness. They are trained in distinctions, segregations, special privileges, as they are trained in their toilet habits. Among the upper classes this training takes on a highly specialized character with subtleties, nuances baffling to those not reared in a bi-racial caste system. As southern children grow older the more intelligent and economically secure among them (and some of the "rebels") tend to reject much of this early conditioning when it is subjected to the checks of common sense and scientific knowledge; and the *more crude* of their race superstitions retire to childhood's shadow to lurk there with other wishful fantasies. But no white child reared among Negroes ever forgets in his heart the sweet power of being "superior." His early belief in white-skin superiority is still there, waiting for the propitious moment of race-strain, to seize its old throne in the middle of reason from which once it was firmly ejected.

Much confusion today among southern liberals is nothing more or less than a surrender under stress to the pull of old childhood patterns of behavior. Even though the mind can not confess it, the emotions have capitulated.

A second cause of confusion springs out of the South's finest tradition: the attempts of individuals to soften for other particular individuals the harsh effects of the southern system. This tradition at its best however is no more than the habit of bestowing largesse of money and spirit upon one's "inferiors." It is a generosity—but it is also the bringing of gifts for which one expects payment in gratitude—"furnish" jotted down in the commissary book of our memories as a debt to be paid not in kind but with very high interest. Many good white people who have helped the Negro are deeply hurt that he will not now repay their help by refraining from embarrassing the white race while it is "in this emergency." Stated so briefly, this may smack of the ridiculous. Rub your mind on it a little and you will feel a nub of truth there. The common complaint, "this is not the right time," betrays the liberal's mistaking for "christmas" the Negro's basic claim to democracy.

A third element in this chaos is the unarticulated fear of reprisal that springs surely from a profound guilt for our treatment of the Negro. We know that the privileged and powerful groups among white men have used the Negro as strike-breaker, as the undertow to pull down and keep down wages, as the post which the poor white can kick when in need of kicking; all these—as well as a strop on which to sharpen their own race pride. It is an old saying that the only way the white man can keep the Negro in the ditch is to stay down there with him. It would be more true to say that the only way the powerful whites have kept the poor whites in the ditch has been by holding the Negro down there *below* them. Whether or not southern liberals have participated directly in this exploitation they have profited directly from it and have been accessories to the fact by their conforming to the southern customs which make such exploitation easy. Hence the unease and fear which we all share, knowing our responsibility for the evils.

This southern race-conditioning, so subtly involved by guilt-feelings, is a profound handicap to reason, crippling the South's efforts toward intelligent action. There are white men in America willing to risk losing the war, if race equality and bread-and-butter democracy are the alternatives. Though few, they are powerful. However, our real danger today lies not in the deliberate sabotage of the war effort by these few but in a falling back of the people upon conditioned reflexes which are not valid responses to the present situation—however successfully they may have served other purposes.

All the Negro wants in this war is to be permitted to do his full share toward winning it, not as an outcaste, an Untouchable, given untouchable chores to attend to, but as a self-respecting decent American citizen functioning usefully within the democratic pattern. All he is now asking is for his Constitutional rights in this democracy. If this be treason . . . as some liberals say . . . the liberals can make the most of it. And are likely to do so—unless the creative way, the constructive, intelligent, and *new* act is attempted.

There is such a way for white men who seek it. It is not an inexorable necessity for us to make one of the deadly and automatic choices: shutting eyes, ears, mouths in appeasement of the demagogues and Negrophobes among us; or asking Negroes to appease their exploiters for white men's sake; or arousing by words the ignorant whites to mob violence.

There is another way: by act, word, newspaper column, editorial, speech, sermon, in quiet reason with friends, public opinion can be created by liberals and labor to accept the Negro in democracy, as public opinion has been created to accept this war. Suggest that the old days have passed; that as war strategy it is the wise thing now, the "hard necessity" perhaps, but the only course to follow both for winning the faith of other peoples across the seas and for strengthening our inner defenses; that it is the inevitable direction which we must take to find a way out of our American troubles and the sooner we take it, the better.

There are ten liberal southern newspaper men who have enough influence to so turn the tide of southern opinion that the people would not seize upon the destructive solution, seeing no other, but would quietly accept the inevitable and creative way if it were pointed out by these leaders. The vast majority of white southerners are neutral people (as is true the world over of people) eager neither to harm nor to help anybody. And being also an unstable people are highly suggestible, easily influenced by leaders. The racists among them, the Negrophobes, the demagogues, some delta planters and a few vested interests who try to fight back the approach of democracy by beating it over the head with the Negro's body might not be appeased by their words. But maybe the Federal government in war time could lay a cool hand on hot tempers.

If the liberals in the South do not turn to the constructive act, if they continue to "solve" deep fundamental conflicts by silence and evasion, pep talks, quiet pressures, or by criticism of Negroes who are attempting to pull their race toward freedom, much of the responsibility for the violence which may result will be theirs—as it has been theirs in the past.

It is well for us all to realize that danger of inciting to race violence does not lie in the *speaking* but in speaking *against* the Negro instead of *for* him, as analyses of race riots show. It would be wise to remember that riots are caused by social and economic conditions, not by the reasoned publicizing of these conditions or attempts to right them. Intelligent southerners cannot afford today to confuse cause with effect. Incitement to violence does not spring from a sane creating of public opinion to deal democratically with the Negro but from inflammatory talk of sex, rape, Pure Womanhood, and "menace."

Liberal southern journalism learned its bitter lesson about rape and womanhood, took an oath of silence, and now fears to break it. It has not yet learned that silence itself in times of race strain may be just as dangerous as sex words. But when the silence is broken, let it be broken by creative reason and justice, not—as has been done already in a few instances—by attacks on the Negro for using his democratic right to free speech. Somehow we must realize that such criticism also encourages violence, for to the ignorant and willful of both races it seems to stamp approval on the making of trouble by white men.

We white liberals cannot in honesty blame the demagogues for stirring up "race trouble"; nor can we in decency accuse Negro leaders of exploiting the war emergency. We do our full share of both by our faintheartedness, our covering up of actual conditions, our personal snobbery, our selfish habit of putting private affairs, state politics, business interests, and desire to be "gentlemen" ahead of deep fundamental human needs.

If we profoundly believe the Negro is as important as the white man, that his happiness and security are as essential as ours, we shall not be so quickly alarmed about "race trouble" by which is meant trouble for the white man. The Negro is always in trouble, a trouble which does not seem to disturb many white people until the contagion spreads from the Quarters to White Town.

Children and Color*

We know a child's personality cannot grow without self-esteem, without feelings of emotional security, without faith in the world's willingness to make room for him to live as a human being.

These are to character what vitamins are to the body. No colored child in our country, however protected within the family, is being given today what his personality needs in order to mature fully and richly. No white child, under the segregation pattern, North or South, can be free of arrogance, hardness of heart, blindness to human needs. The bitter and inescapable fact is that our children in America, white and colored, are growing distorted, twisted personalities within the frame of this segregation which our fears and frustrations have imposed upon them.

.   .   .

I personally would prefer that my own child do without shoes than that he do without the esteem of his fellows, and I would prefer that

* These two selections are taken from speeches before the Fellowship of Southern Churchmen, Raleigh, N.C., March 1943, and the Herald-Tribune Forum, October 1944, respectively.

he never look into a book than that he look down upon another human being. Of course, I want him to know what is in books, but I want much more for him to know what is in men's hearts. This he can never learn unless he looks at others with level eyes. Shoes are important for both white and colored feet—who would deny ! but a child can go barefooted without great harm; he cannot go one day unesteemed by his fellows without injury to his personality. . . .

The Negro wants the four freedoms that the rest of us want and need; but he wants another. Freedom from shame. A freedom that is his profound right to have. The Negro wants freedom from shame for his children, yes; and I want it for ours also! Neither his children nor ours can ever have it as long as segregation is the way of life in America.

HUMANS IN BONDAGE*

In 1943, men dreamed of brotherhood and filled the American calendar with days of rioting and bloodshed, with obscene talk of White Supremacy, with bus fights and death, with smear stories and rumors, with all the fury that destroys men's good feelings for each other and makes understanding difficult.

It is not of these acts of violence that we need to talk now. It is of ourselves. For there is no one reading these words who took part in a race riot, killed a Negro, used the foul words of a Cotton Ed Smith or a Senator Rankin. Men who kill, curse, use foul words in the name of race will kill, curse, use foul words in the name of anything that safely provides outlet for their hate and frustrations. Whether they wear frock coats or overalls, the toga of leadership or the stripes of the chain gang, they are the casualties of a culture which promotes hate more assiduously than love, which makes it so hard for men to live in dignity with each other that, in despair, they tear to

* An article which appeared in the February 15, 1944, issue of *Social Action*, published by the Council for Social Action of the Congregational Christian Churches, New York.

pieces the good along with the bad, hardly knowing one from the other as they search in great hunger for something they lost in their childhood, and which nothing in their culture gave back to them. Theirs is another story—a story beginning with their mothers and fathers and their own childhood, weaving itself in and out of a culture which pressed here, pulled there until there was no way for personalities to fit together in one piece, to find human creative goals to work toward, to feel at ease with themselves.

And we? We are the people who dream the good dreams and let the "bad" people turn them into nightmares. Horrified, yet with a feeling of strange helplessness, we watch their violence, wanting to do something, wanting to stop such things from happening, but blocked from action by paralyzing fear. Our minds fill with compulsive phrases, "You'll do more harm than good. . . . You'll only stir up more trouble. . . . This isn't the right time. . . . You can't change 'customs' quickly, only education. . . ." Or we gasp in relief, "Race prejudice is 'economic,' only by abolishing poverty, etc." (In other words, "Let the unions do it.") We turn away, feeling that there is nothing much that we, personally, can do about it, except perhaps observe Race Relations Day once a year in our churches (though of course that doesn't mean that we must give up segregated churches), or perhaps join an interracial committee (if it isn't too radical), or talk a little about giving "equal opportunity" and a little about housing. Doing the little things so that we can forget that nobody is doing the big things.

All most of us want, deep within us, is to be assured that there will be no more race riots; no more lynchings; no more killings on buses; no more public exhibitions of race obscenities like those of the Rankins, the Cotton Ed Smiths, the Gene Talmadges; no more "flares" of violence calling attention to a way of life in which we all willingly participate and are willing to continue to participate, hoping that the Negroes will be more contented with things as they are and that the psychotic, the delinquent, the criminal will not use "race" as a way of expressing their frustrations.

We who call ourselves the "good" people, the intelligent, even the wise, accept without protest the spiritual lynching of Negroes which goes on around us day by day, in every town, every city, every part of our nation. We accept the quiet killing of self-esteem, the persistent smothering of hope and pride, the deep bruises given the egos of young Negro children; the never-easing humiliations which segregation imposes upon human beings who are not white. We say, almost all white southerners and many white northerners say, that segregation cannot be abolished: whatever is done "for" the Negro must be done under the very system which lynches his spirit and mind every day he is under it.

For most of us are still thinking and feeling as white people. Most of us still want the priorities which we have under the White Supremacy system and we know that when segregation goes, White Supremacy will go with it. Most of us are incapable—having calloused our imaginations with the daily rubbing of one stereotype against another—of realizing what we are saying when we say calmly that "these things must be changed very slowly," that "the Negro has made progress," that "the Negro must 'prove' himself and then he will be 'accepted' by the white man." We drop the heavy yoke of Jim Crow about the Negro's neck and turn away from seeing what it does to the man beneath it. We are saying, in effect, that the system of White Supremacy means so much to us, that the pattern we are living under has given us so many compensations, that we are quite willing for each Negro child born today into the world to have the Jim Crow yoke placed around his shoulders in infancy. We are willing for black children to be humiliated, bruised, hurt daily, subjected to a psychic brutality that would arouse us to fury if our white children were subjected to it—that *has* aroused our fury when it has happened to Jewish children in Germany. We are willing for these things to go on and on, because we cannot bear to change our own feelings, because we cannot endure the thought of tackling the most immediate task before us: the white man and his love for himself and his skin color.

Our trouble is that we cannot feel deeply these words we are saying. Our emotions are blunted where Negroes are concerned. It is as though we had segregated an area in our minds, marked it "colored" and refused our feelings entrance to it. And when we do begin to feel, as lately many of us have been feeling; when there springs up in us that deep, thrilling desire to tear off the steel frame of segregation that is warping both white and black lives and distorting everything fine and good that we prize and believe—then suddenly we are pulled back as if by a chain that will let us go only so far and no farther. The old fear begins its compulsive whispering, *"Yes but this isn't the right time to do it. You'll do only harm, not good."*

As a white southerner, born in a Deep South town whose population was predominantly Negro, reared under the segregation pattern, still living today under it, I know the fears by heart. I know the placid taking for granted of a way of life hideous in its effect upon the spirits of both black and white. I know the dread of change; I know all the rationalizations by which the white man eases his guilt and conserves his feelings of superiority: how he concentrates not on his own problem of white superiority, not on his own obsession with skin color, but instead on the Negro, hoping that somehow the *Negro* can be changed to fit the pattern more harmoniously, as though the white man and his pattern could never be changed. That is what most of us in the South mean when we talk of race relations: a more harmonious adjustment of the Negro to the white man's pattern. And we have sold the idea to the North also.

In times of harmony and of ease, fear grows less, the chain loosens, and we become more amenable to the teachings of Christianity, of democracy, and of science. Even in the Deep South, in times of ease, men grow more "liberal" toward the Negro, feeling then that he can safely be given more privileges. But as tension increases, the old fear increases with it, and action is paralyzed by old taboos against speaking of human relations in terms of human equality. All else may be discussed but segregation; all else but the basic question: *Are* Negroes human, or aren't they? The taboo of silence restrains such talk so effectively that only the hardiest and most independent dare defy it.

This is well demonstrated today in the South by many liberals who in their private lives do not practice the segregation they proclaim in public, who often eat with Negroes (unostentatiously), who, when away from the South—and often while in it—break segregation taboos, but who now insist in public that *for the South the pattern can never be changed.* Moreover, they ostracize and belittle other southerners who dare speak out plainly for a way of life that is Christian and good for southern people. And by this public insistence they tighten the bonds of fear and of deep prejudice in all people; they strengthen the position of demagogues, who have never lacked courage to speak their piece on race hatred; they make it easier for every man of good feeling to regress to less humane ways of behavior. They are not hypocrites, perhaps; not consciously so. They do this, they think, in the name of "expediency." They are not aware of the more profound reasons which make them act, not according to the demands of reality, but according to the demands of unconscious fears and guilt for which they have no name and with which they cannot come to grips.

We need to understand these fears and to gain insight into this problem which all white people share in common. Around this subject of race have gathered the southerner's deepest fears; only about God and sex do we feel as strongly. Religion . . . race . . . sex . . . All that we feel deeply about these matters we began to feel as children. We learned about God, about sex, about race before we began to speak words; and we learned from the people who were dearest to us—our mothers and fathers and nurses. We were trained to feel a certain way about God; a certain way about sex; a certain way about race. We were trained to act out these feelings. The words *race* and *sex* were probably not often used by those who trained us, though we learned early to talk easily of God. But attitudes toward sex and race were more deeply ingrained in our personalities, perhaps, than were our feelings for God. We learned these matters, as children always learn, by feeling deeply about them. We felt profound guilt if we betrayed our learning and we felt as strongly about one of our "lessons" as we did the others.

As we grew older, went to school, read books and travelled, some of us acquired new facts and insights about God, race, and sex . . . but deep within us we tended to feel much as we felt when we were children. We acquired the facade of educated men living in an enlightened world; we behave under most normal conditions as educated, well-informed people should behave. But deep within us we feel much as we felt as children. Any new feeling would seem to our unconscious minds a betrayal of childhood love for our parents.

Much of this we never put into words—not even in our own minds do we think it. And yet it is true that men under strain and pressure tend to regress to earlier, less appropriate feelings. All of us have seen this happen to children. A child who long ago stopped sucking his thumb becomes sick and regresses to thumb-sucking, which represents an earlier and more secure period in his life. We who, in a revolutionary situation, have given up our more "liberal" position of a few years ago are racial thumb-suckers who do not dare now to break the taboos of segregation. And our northern liberal friends have begun to thumb-suck with us. They too are using the rationalizations we have so persuasively taught them—though with far less excuse than southerners whose training in race began earlier and has been carried on more persistently.

Today we talk of one world, of one brotherhood of people. We see the evils of segregation and the harm of our preoccupation with White Superiority; we fear the riots, the murders, and the lynchings. We find it hard to change our obsessive stereotypes and to lose our fear—stronger than the fear of race riots—of meeting old needs in new ways. But we find it easy, as conditions grow hard, to return to our childhood racial feelings, even though they are grotesquely inappropriate to the demands of our world.

Not only have we stereotyped the Negro, but we have stereotyped ourselves and our own feelings. Not only do we need to think of the Negro as human; we need ourselves to become human.

There are, of course, areas in which all of us are "human," in which even delinquents and criminals and the mentally ill function as humans. For there are few people who have not some love left in them, some ability to identify their sympathies with a few other people, some willingness to place the needs of a few, or at least one person, in equal importance with their own. Only the schizophrenic has completely lost his ability to love and to make human identifications. But when we reserve this humanity of ours, this precious quality of love, of tenderness, and of imaginative identification, for only people of our skin color (or of our own family, our own class, or friends) we have split our lives in a way shockingly akin to those sick people whom we call schizophrenics. And we develop—as we whites have developed toward Negroes—a personality picture strongly like theirs of blunted emotions, delusions of persecution, feelings of "aloneness," extreme irritability when efforts are made to change our white ways, and projection of our conflict upon "the Negro" himself (making him the "menace," and the danger). We develop a desire to shut ourselves off not only from the Negro by segregation, but also from all science, all influences that are disturbing to the picture we have made of ourselves and of our "persecutors."

It is not a pleasant picture that I have drawn of my white race. There is not one of us who can take pleasure in thinking of ourselves in a way so disturbing to our complacent self-regard. Yet, if we do not resist it too much, if the aroma of psychiatric words does not offend us too deeply, perhaps we can begin to gain insight into the damage race prejudice has done to our personalities and to white culture. We need to assess this damage, for it is more than poor wages, wasted soil, poverty, race riots; it is more than the damage done to Negroes themselves.

There is a problem facing each of us, black and white, but it is not the "Negro problem." It is the problem, for Negroes, of finding some way to live with white people. It is the problem, for whites, of learning to live with themselves.

During the past two decades much literature has accumulated on the "Negro Problem." Popular magazines, social science journals, and books have printed ten thousand facts and laid them before us.

The average white person now knows a little more than he knew twenty years ago. He knows who the Negro leaders are and their achievements in jazz, song, dance, folk poetry, and the fighting ring. Joe Louis, Marian Anderson, Paul Robeson, W. C. Handy, Cab Calloway, and Paul Lawrence Dunbar have become in the folk-mind racial symbols for a people who can sing, dance, make little verses and big rhythms and fight hard—as well as chop cotton. They know Dr. Carver as a kind of humble scientific-magician, who, always staying in his "place," performed startling tricks with the peanut and the sweet potato. They have heard of Mrs. Mary McLeod Bethune as an elderly majestic black woman who has a powerful way with white folks and who usually gets her way. Many have recently heard of Philip Randolph and Walter White, both of whom wear in the average mind a vague aura of "menace." And lately, they have been seeing in the movies Lena Horne, whose loveliness has crashed like a powerful bomb on the stereotype of the Negro which Stepin Fetchit built up so consistently in the minds of moviegoers for years. As one woman said in a theater in a small Georgia town, "Why, she isn't a nigger any more than I am! What is she?"

There is still little known generally about Negroes who are distinguished scientists, lawyers, economists, writers, editors, artists, sculptors, actors, doctors, and religious and labor leaders, but information about them is now available in many libraries. Such knowledge is gradually, though far too slowly, wearing down old images of the childlike-laughing-singing-dancing-fighting-clowning-lying Negro.

It was inevitable that segregation should create such stereotypes. When great barriers are thrown up between people who are living side by side, when normal human relationships between those who daily see each other are made not only difficult but taboo by custom and law, curiosity grows. Little peekholes have been made in this wall of segregation; here and there secret doors allow a furtive passing back and forth. And lately whites and blacks have been throwing their books over the wall to each other. Yet, until recent years, there have been few facts to feed this curiosity upon, and it has had to feed upon legends, myths, and fantasies.

Although the basic stereotypes had their origin in the South, they have also been accepted in the North. Most Americans are familiar with that strange story white folks used to tell themselves (and unfortunately still tell) about colored folks.

> The Negro was created by God to be a hewer of wood and a drawer of water. He was set aside by the Lord to serve the white man and to keep him in ease and comfort. Because the white man needs to laugh, God made the black man funny. He gave him a talent for singing and dancing, and a gift for making "spirituals" so that the white man could have some music and gaiety and religious sentiment in his life as well as a bank account. God also made the black man childlike and simple and by nature contented (except when Yankee trouble-makers, white and black, come around!). And this has been fine for the white man, since it has caused the Negro to be so easily "managed."

This, of course, is the story about the Good Negro. The Bad Negro's story is different:

> The Bad Negro uses a razor blade with a skill that arouses awe if you are out of reach and terror if you are in its orbit. He is easily angered, easily made drunk, and will always attempt to rape any unprotected white woman. He "talks back" to white folks and has to be kept in his place—and if he is too difficult, this place naturally becomes a noose hanging from an old cypress. All Negroes are liars, lazy, and loud-mouthed.

Most of us are familiar with these stories and try to smile when we hear them, but with no pleasure in the smiling, for we remember that there are still people who believe them.

White people are not as familiar with the story southern Negroes have told themselves about white folks—a story that seems to linger on more pesistently among literate Negroes in the North than in the South. The story goes like this:

> The white man in the South is a chronic lyncher. He seizes every opportunity to stage a lynching bee, which his wife and children often attend as delighted spectators. Sometimes the children are given chopped-off toes, etc., for souvenirs of the festive occasion. All white

folks are arrogant and cruel and potential killers who often talk fine talk about "loving" but spend their lives cheating and shaming Negroes. All white men have children by Negro women and many of the white people in the South who call themselves "white" are really part Negro. All white folks are liars, and lazy and rude.

Many Negroes tell this story with zest and too many actually believe it. Most southern whites have never heard it and are incredulous and hurt when they discover that southern Negroes entertain such ideas about them. To whites and Negroes of other regions this story does not seem difficult to accept.

The stereotypes are almost endless. There is the classic: "Nobody understands the Negro like the white southerner." And its twin: "We in the South love the Negro and he loves us; it's only when agitators, etc., etc."

There are the phrases: "nigger lover," "northern agitators," "carpet-bagger," "Uncle Toms," "handkerchief heads"—all of which are verbal weapons used in intra-racial warfare, for never has there been, nor is there now any unity among white folks about their feelings for Negroes or among Negroes about their feelings for white folks.

There are the fixed ideas: "Negroes are primitive. . . . After all they have done pretty well when you consider they are only 300 years from savagery." . . . "Negroes don't want to be treated as white folks. They will lose their respect for you if you treat them as equals."

There is the odd assortment of fantasies about physiology and physiognomy: "Round sloping heads indicate low mentality." . . . "Strong body odors are found only among Negroes." . . . "One drop of black blood, etc. . . ." There are also the more detailed accounts of esoteric sex practices and sadistic performances which each group relates about the other. They are stereotypes as vulgar, as crude and as distorted as chalk drawings scribbled by children on outhouses— and created from the same motives! They tell us nothing about the subject, but much about the artist who made them. And for that reason these racial stereotypes, under analysis, yield us knowledge of fantasies, which white and black people have about each other—and themselves.

A magazine recently told this story: A young boy returned from school with a drawing which he proudly showed his mother. A tactful person, she looked at it a long time trying to decide what the drawing was about. Finally, unable to decide, she gently said, "It is very intresting, Son, but—what is it?" "A Jap," he said triumphantly. "A Japanese?" "Yes'm." "But you have never seen a Japanese, have you?" "No, ma'am," the youngster said, "I've never seen a Japanese, so I thought I'd draw one to see what he looks like."

Drawing pictures of what we have never seen "so we can know what it looks like" is an old human habit, not limited to children. For decades, white people and colored people have been drawing such pictures of each other. It is hard now for them to believe their senses when they meet as actual human beings.

Old stereotypes can be broken in pieces by ten thousand facts told in ten thousand ways through radio, movies, books, newspapers, the theater, speeches; and new and more authentic stereotypes can be substituted for them. This is a desirable and even urgent thing to do when minds are cluttered with false images. Yet it is well to remember that if we want to change stereotypes into real human beings, nothing but meeting each other, nothing but personal relationships can do it. One may call a ragweed a rose and later be told by authorities that it is not a rose at all. But until one sees a rose, experiences a rose, then experiences hundreds of roses and likes some of them, one does not really know what roses are.

The loss of common sense in human relations is a natural result of the socially destructive and mentally unhealthful pattern of segregating one group of people from another. Whether people are separated by sex or age, by color or wage differences, by language or talents, the results are inevitably the same: a blurring of images takes place, fantasies are substituted for reality and a creeping paralysis of anxiety makes change seem impossible.

Although segregation has made human relationships most difficult, nothing but human relationships can break down segregation.

Nothing else can change the habit of thinking in stereotypes about each other, and remove the deeply entrenched, irrational fears that such thinking has created. Laws may be removed from statute books (although they will not be until enough people form relationships despite the laws, and insist upon their removal), but the custom of racial segregation will still isolate people from each other unless individuals build personal bridges across the chasm, build more and more bridges, until finally there is no more separation. The two processes of breaking down segregation and building up new human relations must go on simultaneously. Neither has priority over the other.

Perhaps the most important thing any of us can do is to change our own feelings about people who are superficially different from ourselves, whether in the color of their skin, in religion, or in political ideologies. We can learn to identify ourselves more skillfully with people not made in our exact image. This is not an easy thing to learn after attitudes and feelings have become rigid. It is the "unfinished business" of emotional maturity—and any observer can see how much of this "unfinished business" is lying around in white personalities.

It is as difficult as lifting one's self by one's own bootstraps, but human beings are capable of bootstrap dexterity, as all civilization reminds us. If we realize the need for change, if we want to change, we *can* change—except those of us who are mentally ill, or whose personalities have no more growth in them.

Sometimes reading books will help us. They will stir torpid imaginations, will give us sharp realizations of our failings, of the need of others, and of the danger that our inertia creates. For those who find the written word of emotional and intellectual value, reading will arouse desire for change and give the strength to make it.

Others need comradeship in their undertaking, need the encouragement which comes from knowing that one is not alone. For often democratic racial action means a long struggle between Christian conscience and white culture. One needs at least the cushion of a sympathetic group to ease the pain of continuous conflict. However limited the work of interracial committees may be, this "together-ness" is a valuable secondary gain of such group activities. Labor unions, racial and civil liberties groups, all have their function of bringing individuals together for a common purpose—all pay compound interest on one's investment of courage. So don't be afraid to be a "joiner"—if you are joining a project worth doing.

Meet and form friendships with individuals of other racial groups. This does not "just happen." North or South, we must make it happen. Labor unions may be one way if your union is not segregated. Defense work may give you the opportunity, if you will take it. "American Common" in New York is a place where people of all groups may meet for congenial purposes. There should be a half dozen "American Commons" in every city. Universities in the North often have inter-cultural groups and classes where friendships may be formed and students of different races may meet each other. In the South it is more difficult. There are Negro college campuses where well-bred white people are usually welcomed. There are interracial committees.

There are Negro churches which cordially accept white visitors with sincerity of purpose. Though few white churches in the South will make a Negro feel comfortable. There are likewise few churches in the North where whites and Negroes mingle freely in worship and brotherhood. But many women's church groups, North and South, do have occasional interracial gatherings and these are good starting-places for the development of friendships.

There are Other Ways:

1. *Exchange letters with individuals of other racial groups.* This is something that white and colored people, North and South, can do without losing jobs, prestige, or incurring the hostilities of one's neighbors. Such correspondence carried on for several years will increase sympathies and esteem and strengthen bonds of friendship. If, for instance, one thousand white southern women corresponded frequently with one thousand colored southern women over a period of years, one could reasonably expect little

miracles of racial democracy to begin popping up all over Dixie—or Detroit! Often the simple, undramatic, personal act brings about great change in people's feelings. When feelings change, customs change also.

2. *A function of interracial committees can usefully be that of bringing congenial men and women of both races together.* It is quite possible that such a group could act as a "Racial Register" for those who express a desire to meet interesting individuals of other races. All interracial committees in the South would be far more valuable to their community if they had a center where members of racial groups felt free to come and go, to meet for casual chats or more important interviews. A place in a church might be set aside for this purpose or if the churches are afraid, perhaps a labor union might have courage to offer its hospitality! It is not a wholly fantastic idea, and might be workable if a little thought were given to it. (It would not of course be easy. Nothing that promotes racial democracy in the South is going to be easy. We must face that. On the other hand, neither will it be "dangerous," or "cause more trouble," or produce that race riot which seems to be always around the corner in southern minds.) It would be less difficult to arrange such a center in a northern city or town, and it is as greatly needed there as in the South.

3. *Small, quiet gatherings.* It is very important that people meet in each other's homes. Have lunch together. Sit in the living-room and talk together. Invite a friend of another race in for dinner with the family. We have no Gestapo in America to invade the privacy of our homes and punish us for civilized and Christian tastes. Yet we make a Gestapo of our fears and become cowards at the sound of our own heart-beat, mistaking it for the heavy clump clump of disaster. Not even in the South is it "dangerous" for whites and Negroes to have each other in their homes, if they wish it. Quiet, tactful, dignified arrangements are necessary but such small social meetings, if deftly planned, will not become the high explosives that an anxiety-burdened folk-imagination has

declared them to be. Whatever the danger, it is small compared to the compensation of knowing that one is helping create a Christian democratic culture.

4. *Pressures and protests.* Letters will help create a new public opinion about matters which we too often push out of our minds, believing we are helpless to do anything about them. Letters to city officials, newspapers, radio stations, state and national officials do have their effect.

It is important to write letters commending people for their efforts to create a better social climate. One busy advertising executive writes five such letters each week, praising men and women throughout the country for their effective work in racial, economic, and religous fields. Recently, Virginius Dabney, editor of the *Richmond Times-Dispatch*, took a stand against segregation on buses, street-cars, and trains in Virginia. If he receives many letters of commendation it will naturally encourage him and will have much to do with influencing other southern editors to follow his example.

Most inflammation of public opinion against the colored peoples stems directly from demagogues and economic powers (sometimes industry, sometimes labor) to whose immediate advantage is the keeping alive of fear and distrust in men's minds. The counter-pressures will have to come from individuals and small groups of citizens (with no great powers) who will take the trouble to put in their "two cents' worth" for democracy and Christianity. Five letters a week, commending the good things and criticizing the bad, would be a valuable contribution for anyone to make at this time. Of course it would be a bit of trouble, but it would change public opinion and cause vested groups to do some thinking.

5. *Insist that Negro characters in movies be more intelligent and attractive,* that old stereotypes be minimized, such as the lazy houseboy, the curtseying mammy, and the ignorant and superstitious farm hand (true as some of these stereotypes still are in many places). Urge producers to include Negroes and whites in

the same cast on equal basis, as the theater has done for so long. A step in this direction would be a serious drama with an all-Negro cast, where fresh types such as the college Negro, the serious worker, the professional man, and the person of subtlety, intelligence, and individuality are used. Such a picture though still in the segregated pattern would be a move away from the old stock characters. There is no influence more potent for racial democracy than movies.

6. *Group visits.* The group visit is a creative way of changing men's ideas and actions. It has not been used enough by people of good will and intelligence, who do not seem to realize its potency, or else consider it too much trouble. Small committees, even an individual, can call on officials of government, radio stations, newspapers, churches, judges and educational leaders and discuss situations which need clearing up. Hostilities are minimized this way, new understandings arise, and a pooling of efforts often results. It is not very dramatic: there are no fights or fireworks. It is a civilized, intelligent method that fits a philosophy of good means to produce good ends. Whether good results are accomplished depends upon how many visits are paid and who pays them. One such visit a month would be a nice score to chalk up on the side of your creative efforts.

7. *Join organizations.* There are so many. Investigate them carefully, then join those whose leaders are thoughtful, intelligent people working for good purposes. Support them by your money, your letters, and your willingness to help with their programs.
Some unions are worthy of your support, others are not. Strong, mature, democratic unions and strong cooperatives are two vital and creative movements in America today. Both need support. Study them; encourage them; support their good leaders, help oust the bad ones, and give unions and cooperatives a chance to grow strong.

8. *Common sense things to do.* Work for the abolition of the poll tax and the white primary; for non-segregation in the armed forces,

for a voluntary mixed regiment; for no discrimination in industrial jobs or labor unions; for a federal law against lynching; for federal aid in education; for the removal of segregation laws from southern states; for better housing, and non-segregated housing; for better health facilities for Negroes and whites; and for more play-grounds. All of these will help the Negro and the white man. Write letters and speak out against segregation in transportation and churches. Patronize and encourage unsegregated restaurants and hotels in the North. Work for them in the South. Work for unsegregated hospitals, apartment houses, and schools. Work for justice in the courts, regardless of race, religion, sex, or economic status.

And pay your cook more wages, shorten her hours, treat her with consideration. Give her job human prestige.

Try to forget that you are white. It will be hard, but try. For one day test your words, your statements, your actions in the house, on the streets, in your work and in public places. Live on the assumption that your skin color does not give you any priorities. The day may be interesting to you and to your Negro friends.

9. *Don'ts for whites.* Don't get mad if Negroes do not gush with appreciation for your civilized, democratic efforts. They will probably overpay you in gratitude; but remember they don't "owe" you anything. You owe it to yourself to be sane and civilized, and you owe it to your family and your culture.

Don't let your habit of segregated language trip you up with the phrase "you people." Most Negroes don't like it. Don't criticize Negroes in the white newspapers. It is rotten sportsmanship and does nothing but reinforce white prejudice. Write letters directly to the Negroes you wish to criticize; criticize the Negro press in the Negro press, where it will be read by the people for whom it is intended. Avoid telling derogatory stories about Negroes, even when they are intrinsically funny.

There is no easy way these days to protect our children from receiving a severe color-conditioning. Front seats for white folks;

WHITE-COLORED warnings as conspicuous as road signs over doors (over almost all southern doors); segregated housing, segregated hotels, apartment houses, restaurants, and hospitals (North and South); racial jokes, racial smear words; "Relocation Centers" for our Japanese-descended American citizens (many of which with grim relevancy are placed in a color-prejudiced South); Jim Crow on buses, trains, street-cars, and theaters; obvious discrimination in the armed services and industry—all are cultural pressures shaping the child's feelings about himself and others. How can any child escape the effect of these pressures? The only answer is found in counter-pressures and the home. The home and parental training can offset this color culture if parents desire to keep the minds of their children sane and human.

*　*　*

There is no easy way to train our children to form good human relationships, but there are ways:

1. We can train children by our own attitudes and acts to respect other people and their needs regardless of color, religion, economic status, or sex.

*　*　*

2. We can train children not to think themselves too important. This can be done in simple, casual, humorous ways by reminding them that no one is the center of the universe after he learns to walk and talk. You can't *be* the center, unless you *stay* there. The center isn't going to move around with you. Children respond eagerly to the basic idea of growing up—of steady growth toward emotional maturity as something moral and "right" and fun to work toward. It is easy to get them to see emotional growth as a process of including more and more people in one's life and of making more and more identifications with their feelings and needs.

If a child is wisely guided through his early family adjustments his emotional growth is not likely to be stopped on the infantile level of self-love and self-importance, nor is he likely to continue to crave a feeling of superiority. We would not expect him to crave candy all the time if he had plenty of good food and affection. Racial prejudice, if a persisting trait in the personality, suggests an abnormal appetite for self-importance, which the wise parent will consider a danger signal.

* * *

In the case of the Negro child, wise guidance gives him a stability and a psychic security that will stand him well against discriminating actions that often hinder the development of a stable personality.

It is possible to show children while they are quite young that segregation is not only a peculiar attitude of white people toward Negroes, or a southern custom that "must change very slowly"; segregation is basically the method everybody uses to shut himself off from reality when he feels threatened by a danger he cannot explain. It is a retreat toward self-love and infantilism, toward (as the psychiatrists would say) death. In shutting one's eyes to keep from seeing a danger, one shuts out the sight of danger, but shuts out the whole world with it—a process that makes schizophrenics of some men and Negro-phobes of others.

The habit of segregating one's self from something one fears or feels guilty about is too dangerous to encourage in any child—as dangerous to his mind and emotions as is the marijuana habit. It is odd that parents, who would go into a panic if they saw their child smoking marijuana, accept the whole racial and religious segregation pattern of life with no protest.

3. We can make certain that a child's day has in it ample opportunity for him to get rid of his hate and aggression, not only by interesting play and work but by giving him something to hate that needs to be hated, something to fight for that needs to be fought for—so that he will not have to hate and fight people. Hobbies, opportunity to develop talents, something to build up, something to tear down—all are outlets for a hate that is too easily, in a narcissistic culture, turned against those superficially different from ourselves.

4. We can give our children opportunities to play and work with other children on terms of equality. In many parts of the country unsegregated nursery and public schools, unsegregated Boy Scout and Girl Scout troops, and unsegregated clubs and playgrounds can provide opportunities. In the South it will not be as easy. But even there, children of other races and religions can be invited to the home, if these matters are wisely handled.

5. Frank discussions with children about racial customs and racial prejudices do good, not harm—if the discussions take place in an atmosphere of good-will and sympathy, and if the discussions suggest opportunities for improvement and progress. If a child can name a thing and discuss it with adults, it loses its character of menace, and he loses a persuasive anxiety about it. Such a discussion should be followed by some kind of action toward "making things better." Genuine understanding between a white and a colored child would ease for the colored child the personality shocks and bruises he is likely to receive later from whites who are not his friends. And it would give the white child a feeling of comradeship and sympathy not easily forgotten.

There is probably no Christian minister who would attempt to defend racial segregation as Christian. Yet today segregation is a fact which is taken for granted in most churches, South and North.

Not many decades ago, a minister directed his people not only through the Order of Worship but also through all the intricate paths of righteousness. He boldly showed them the map to Heaven and they believed he knew all the road signs. They listened when he said, "This road leads to destruction; this is the highway to hell. This steep, tortuous path is the only way to life everlasting"; and they meekly assented when he struck names off the church register because feet had detoured among primroses.

They were perhaps naive congregations, and their preachers were Men of God who had in their own personalities more than a touch of the fire-and-brimstone with which they threatened their hearers. They were men sometimes misinformed, sometimes crude, often simple and lovable, perhaps sadistic, perhaps too pleasure-hating, but generally men of power. And they were not afraid. Whatever they believed, they said. They believed they knew more than their church members; they felt close to God, and their words were a curious mixture of humility and arrogance as they told their listeners what was right and what was wrong. They were God's Servants and leaders of men.

Last week a minister of one of the South's large churches said he would like to invite a Negro preacher to take his pulpit on Race Relations Sunday but "my congregation would not stand for it." A month ago a group of ministers and laymen considered inviting a Negro to speak to them at their Monday luncheon but decided against it "for old Mrs. So-and-So (a church trustee) will hear of it and there will be trouble." Another minister was asked: "How can you justify segregation in the church with Christian teachings?" He smiled and said, "You are an idealist, aren't you? Well," he sighed, "I happen to be a realist. I deal in realities. I don't justify segregation, but I know my southern people."

Where are our brave Men of God? Our leaders?

Today our congregations are more sophisticated and literate. Our ministers are also more sophisticated and literate—and they know their people. Many of them would like to take a stand against segregation. They would like to practice brotherhood but they fear they will lose their churches. They fear they will offend the wealthy members on whose contributions they depend so heavily. They fear there will be "bad publicity." They fear their usefulness will be curtailed. They fear.

Like the rest of us, they are afraid to do right.

It is a bitter thing to see God's Servants become hired men of the congregation, meekly taking orders from local prejudices, genuflecting not to the teachings of Jesus but to Mrs. So-and-So's notions about Negroes, and turning over the temple to money-changers.

There are those, of course, who are different: North and South, there are brave men who preach and attempt to practice the teachings of Jesus with no regard for the consequences to themselves.

Some of these by virtue of great personal gifts still hold their large congregations; some have lost their pulpits; others, once ministers of large city churches, are now pastors of small rural charges. But they are not sad men for they have no fear.

There is need for courage now, but few have it, in pew or pulpit. How can we get it back? Perhaps if we were a little less fearful we could believe that God would give it to us for the asking. Some of us, weary of our craven spirits, would like to believe that. For never was there a time when preaching could be such an adventure. Never a time when the church has had such a challenging, difficult task before it. Never has the world so needed what Christianity can give it.

Once this writer lived in China and worked in a mission school. Though she saw many mistakes made by missionaries, many instances of stupidity and ignorance, much blind following of inappropriate American cultural patterns, she never saw one act of fear. The missionaries have more courage than we have at home.

Fear is more pervasive in the South than in the North, more deeply rooted, the tasks harder and the need greater. The men who fill this need will suffer for their beliefs and the speaking of them. In the North, to get rid of segregation will be less hard and less demanding of sacrifice. Perhaps for this reason the North should take the leadership in making brotherhood a reality in the churches. And yet it must be done in the South too. North and South must work together. And ministers must unite to give themselves the strength to drive out their fear.

Get rid of segregation in our churches and our pulpits. Whether slowly or quickly done, we must get rid of it. We must preach for brotherhood and against white pride. We must destroy racial superstitions and take our stand against discrimination. We must insist that anyone, of whatever race, be welcomed. We must make the church once more a sanctuary for those who need peace. Even in the Deep South a Negro should feel at home in any church, feel free to relax there, free to worship there, free to mingle in fellowship with other Christians.

In the North, radical changes can be made quickly. Indeed it is difficult for a southerner to see any real obstacle in the way of all churches in the North declaring that the days of segregation are over.

In the South, the taboo of associating with Negroes on a basis of human equality is almost as strong as the taboo against incest. Only by summoning the aid of science, of psychiatry, of Christianity, of great world forces can new fear be built up to take the place of the old fear. The preachers can help develop this new fear—not fear of hell (which used to be a good weapon for the old preachers in their battles for Righteousness) but fear of self-destruction in this life; fear of the damage which hate and arrogance do to minds and emotions, and fear of the consequences for individual men and the human race if white people don't find their place in the earth's family and stay there. As for love . . . once preachers preached about it, and then lost their own belief in its magic. But psychiatrists have rediscovered it. They are telling us that love is powerful medicine in emotional illness, as specific for many mental "infections" as penicillin for physical ailments. Perhaps the church will take courage from science and once more declare its faith in the love of God and man.

Ways can be found, in the South, one by one. Such simple things as year-round interracial ministerial groups would be a first step. Frequent exchange of pulpits (or even congregations) between white and Negro ministers is another. Interracial groups of women working on a common project which the community needs for its children is a third possibility. Joint worship services may be held on special days: on Christmas and Race Relations Day, and an outdoor Easter sunrise service with white and Negro ministers and choirs—all these might be good ways for southerners to begin meeting together in worship. There are ways of bringing the children together through special ceremonies. A white and Negro church might undertake together a nursery school for children, a playground in a neighborhood where delinquency is high, or a health center for children and mothers.

It is not difficult to find ways to come together when people want to be with one another.

This criticism of the church, a criticism more relevant for southern than for northern churches but perhaps to some degree valid for both, is made with sympathy and with full understanding of the exactions and the distortion white culture has imposed upon Christianity. It is made with deep appreciation of how difficult courage is in every day life; how heavy is the psychic burden of speaking of love and brotherhood to those who stop their ears from the hearing.

The church must dream a new dream. But before this dream can become a reality, not only the preacher must dream it but the congregation also. The struggle between conscience and culture is too severe for men to bear alone.

*　*　*

TEN YEARS FROM TODAY[*]

Ten years from today, racial segregation as a legal way of life will be gone from Dixie. Although signs will still be nailed to a few people's minds and hearts, the signs over doors, those words WHITE and COLORED that have cheapened democracy throughout the world will be down.

A prophet is not needed to make this forecast. Anyone who looks closely at recent events here in the South and measures them against world events will know that the future holds no place in it for the philosophy and practice of segregation. Whether segregation takes the form of the iron curtain as it does in communist countries, or the familiar Jim Crow practices that we know in the South, or those severe restrictions that make up the pattern of life in South Africa, it is a belief, an act of the past which the future cannot use.

Ten years ago, neither you nor I would have thought this change could take place so quickly. Do you remember the deep sense of hopelessness, the anxiety, the fear that our young Negro GIs felt at

[*] Commencement address at Kentucky State College, June 5, 1951.

that time as they were being conscripted into the armed services? Do you remember—but who could forget!—how they tried to stifle their bitterness as they were called upon to defend their second-class citizenship? It was a sad and hard ordeal that these men experienced in 1941—your older brothers, your fathers, your uncles, perhaps even a few of you—a test of the human spirit's capacity to love and believe in and defend a country that withheld from them, because of color, their deepest right: the right to be fully accepted as citizens and as human beings.

The Negroes of America measured up to that test with a courage and wisdom that grew out of their capacity for hope, out of their recognition that democracy, despite its failures in regard to them, had yet succeeded in giving the greatest freedom to the largest group of people of any system of government that the world has ever known. Despite its Jim Crow practices, its blindness about race, it had given its citizens more work, higher living standards, more education, more freedom of speech and thought and belief, and *more flexible means of expressing their differences and calling attention to and meeting their needs,* than had any other government in man's history.

It is a very important thing for us to remember today, that no government can *make men good;* even God cannot do that. What democracy can and does do is to protect men's right to make themselves as good as they want to be. No government can rid men of poverty, or of ill health or of ignorance. What democracy does—and no other form of government has ever done more—is to protect its citizens' right to rid themselves of poverty and ill health and ignorance; and to safeguard its people's capacity for human growth. When it fails to do this—and it has failed in regard to the Negro group too often, and has failed in regard to other groups—it yet has within its organism *the potentials for correcting its own failures.* Democracy is based on the laws of organic growth and organic health and these laws cannot be improved upon.

It was a hard thing for Negroes in the armed services in 1941 and 1942 to hold on to this belief in the democratic process, with the

Rankins and the Talmadges and the Bilbos shouting in their ears words that were enough to make any man lose his courage. But they held stubbornly to their faith and many of them gave their lives for it on faraway Pacific islands. They died on those beaches and in the hills and in strange European cities for something they had never had but which they knew *you* would have, some day. And today, other young men are dying for it in Korea, knowing now that the dream is at last coming true for you.

Their faith was justified. The walls of segregation are crumbling now. Crumbling so fast that it is not possible to keep up with the changes happening every day in the little towns of Dixie and in the cities, sometimes blazing out in signs big enough for the whole world to see, sometimes quietly working in men's hearts. Yes, the walls are falling.

Let us quickly remind ourselves of some of the barriers that are already down:

Hundreds of Negro students are now in southern white colleges and universities. The figure is often placed as high as a thousand. And there has been no tension on the campuses of these schools, despite the demagogues' warnings that violence would come, were this to happen. Well, it has happened and there has been no violence. It is going to happen more and more until every state school and university in the South opens its doors to students regardless of their color. I believe, in less than five years, all our graduate and undergraduate schools will be open to Negroes and whites. Five years? Let's make it three—I doubt that even my state of Georgia can hold out three years.

Now as these state colleges open, our private colleges should open also—especially our schools supported by the churches. That is the way of democracy. Public opinion must always change a little faster than do the laws. It is right that the theological schools should open *now*, since they claim to train Christian leaders—not followers, but leaders. And it is good to note that many of the Catholic schools have opened their doors to Negroes, and a few, a very few, of the Protestant schools—among them the Baptist Seminary at Louisville, Kentucky—have opened to both races.

Where else are the walls coming down? In interstate travel, changes have come rather swiftly. Because of the old taboo about eating, we southerners know that the abolition of restrictions in dining cars is a profound cultural change. Today, it is a pleasant thing to report that southerners are now watching each other eat as they travel through Dixie and no one has felt violent about it, no one has fainted, no one has had acute indigestion. The sanity that our southern people possess has prevailed.

This basic sanity of our people needs to be stressed. We have of course our share of the mentally ill and delinquent and our share of the perverse and our share of potential criminals. But it is a small percentage, I think. Yet the politicians and the Klansmen and yes, a few timid newspaper editors, have given the world the impression that southerners are a violent, unstable people unable to take criticism, unable to change even when change is necessary for survival. It is a curious thing to me: this lack of faith in the good sense of our people which not only politicians express but sometimes even the most intelligent of our leaders. They have forecast violence and riots whenever change has been suggested—as if our southern people are unable to behave with dignity and sanity. And these dire prophecies have sometimes scared northern leaders too—among them many editors and writers. This discouraging suggestion that southern people are too neurotic to accept change is of course used as a weapon—and it has been one powerful enough, often, to restrain many people of good will from doing what they know is right. It is working less well today because the South has already, within the past two years, proved this libel against its basic sanity false.

We are changing down here, changing rapidly, and without violence. Let us name quickly other changes:

Negro policemen on nearly every southern city police force; Negro trained nurses fully integrated now into the national association of graduate nurses with their full rights as to equal salaries, etc., protected; Negroes on civic boards of many southern cities—the latest city to elect a Negro representative to a city board is Greensboro, N.C. The masks are off of the Klan in Georgia, in South Carolina, in Florida, in other southern states also. Now, without secrecy, the

Klan will soon die out. Not only the new laws and the stripping off of those pillowcases but the outspoken disapproval of the Klan by nearly all educated white persons in the South make their further activities almost an impossibility.

More than 750,000 Negroes voted in recent elections in the South. Indications are that a million and a half will vote in 1952. There has been violence, now and then; a few Negroes have been killed or beaten up when attempting to vote. But always this violence comes where there are violent Negro-hating politicians stirring up the hate feelings of the people.

Many southern libraries have opened their research departments to Negro scholars. A few city libraries have opened their front doors to all citizens who want to read, regardless of race.

Unsegregated audiences are becoming more and more wide-spread. I have spoken to many unsegregated southern audiences within the past year and I am sure that other speakers have also.

In national sports, we have grown used to seeing Negroes and whites playing together. That is almost an old story now.

And yet, these changes may seem small—set against the tight rigid system of segregation in the South as you and I who were born here, know it. There is still so much to be done. Still so many barriers that seem as solid as concrete. But we must remember that each change is like a hole in a dam; the waters are pouring through; the hole is getting larger and larger; there is no way to plug it now, and soon the old dam will topple. There is no way—because the waters of change are in flood the world over.

Segregation in the South has been like a primitive taboo—different quantitatively and qualitatively, I think, from segregation in the North. A taboo says: *if you do this, you will die or those you love will die. Great disaster will befall you.* A taboo says: *you must never question you must simply obey.* A taboo's magic lies always in its ability to keep every one from daring to break it or talk about breaking it. If one person dares to question it aloud; if two question, three, four—ah, then, the magic no longer "works." Those who support segregation have depended upon fear and silence to keep it strong in the South. Now the old silence is gone. Hundreds of men and women are saying their deep beliefs out loud. The old cliché, said so often in speeches and editorials, that "only a fool would question segregation," is not being heard much, this spring, in Dixie. It is a statement made not even by the dixiecrats. For we have grown a bountiful crop of "fools" lately who are questioning segregation not only in their letters to the press, and in speeches, but in casual conversations, everywhere.

This breaking of the old conspiracy of silence in the South is big news, for when men talk they change. Philosophers have often said that man is the only animal who talks to himself. He is certainly the only animal who talks *about* himself, about his past, his feelings, his dreams, his future. And he is the only animal who can change himself. Because he is a talking animal, he can talk about his dreams, and talking about his dreams makes him want those dreams to come true, and wanting those dreams to come true gives him the power to change himself, to draw upon hidden potentialities for growth within himself.

Dreaming, talking, acting: this is the way that free men bring change about, whether it is change within themselves or within their culture or laws.

These changes taking place in the South are good news for you and me—but not for everybody. Certainly not for the politicians. The old-line politician has used racial fears so long that without this powerful weapon he feels politically castrated. What will he do? It has been so much easier to win votes by arousing anxieties and then promising to allay these false anxieties, than it has been to deal with the rational needs of people. Part of the answer is that some of these old politicians will have to go home and h'ist their feet up on the porch railing and think of the past that is no more, of those lush meadows of fear and hate and ignorance that they used to exploit so profitably. Fortunately, there are young intelligent socially aware politicians who will take their places: men like Estes Kefauver. But some of these old-line politicos are rather durable. Some of them will wet their finger, hold it up to the breeze, and well, you know—just get converted overnight to the new idea of a changing South. They cannot make the future but they are realists enough to get in step with the future when it twists their elbows.

In addition to the old-line politicians, there are white and colored people who do not want to give up segregation because they make money off of our Jim Crow life. Negro business leaders of the South are, some of them, very sad about segregation going. They've grown rich in this segregated system. But they should remember that all of us are still going to die someday—and all of us still need insurance, maybe more of it than ever, just now. Even if we are unsegregated, business will still be good! There are white rural landlords in the backward counties who are unhappy about this too, and certain white real estate groups in the North, and absentee landlords in the North—and a few southern industrialists who want to control the race-baiting politicians.

But there are others also, white and colored, closer to you and me, who do not want to give up segregation because they have deep psychological reasons for clinging to it. It has become a part of their personal defense system against the world. A part of mine, too, perhaps, and of yours. The ego's job in the human personality is to work, to get things done, to create and organize and carry through its purposes, but part of its job is to defend the personality against hurts from both the outside and inside worlds.

Racial segregation has been a strong wall behind which weak egos have hidden for a long time. A white man who feels inferior, who can add up more failures than successes in his public and private life craves the feeling of superiority which his white skin has given him in our culture. Sometimes it has been all he has had. A Negro who has been frustrated in his home, who did not get a good emotional start as a child, who has also felt oppression in its many painful Jim Crow forms, has leaned so hard on his hatred of white people and on the withdrawal which this wall of segregation has made possible, that he is going to feel torn loose from his moorings when segregation disappears, and with it much of the racial humiliation which has justified his hate—at least, to his own conscience. Whom is the Negro going to hate when the white man is no longer his enemy? On whom can he blame his frustrations and failures? Whom is the white man going to feel "superior to" when Negroes are fully accepted as citizens and human beings? Whom is he going to hurt, when he wants to hurt somebody? Whom is he going to shun, when he wants to withdraw?

These are real and important questions—and a lot of individuals in Dixie are going to have to learn to answer them. For the truth is, many southerners have used the walls of segregation so long to lean on psychologically that they will find it very hard to stand on their own two feet as human beings, when the walls go. It is going to be hard for every one of us, no matter how stable and objective, to create within our own minds the new image of ourselves as mature human beings. We have been "white" and "colored" so long . . .

This loss of one's old psychic defenses, one's old image of the self, is the price that mankind pays and has always paid for profound cultural change. And this loss is often the cause of the violence that change sometimes brings forth.

It is very important, therefore, for us to understand that these changes now taking place in our culture cannot take place harmoniously without equal changes taking place within men's hearts and minds. It is important that we remember, also, that when a man gives up something, even old defenses, he is not going to feel good unless he has something equal, or better, returned to him. This is the bargain which each human being makes with his own personality; this is the bargain a man makes with his family, his government, his culture, and even with his religion. These are the terms of real and lasting peace, whether it be peace of mind or soul, or peace between nations, classes, or races.

We have two big jobs ahead of us, now that profound changes are taking place in our South, now that segregation is crumbling. The first job is to hasten the crumbling, for *time is important.* Walls are not only falling in the South, they are falling everywhere, and American democracy can win the imagination of the world only by showing the world that within the strongest democracy on earth all of its citizens have been accepted and given their rights.

Our second job is a very important one also. And I stress it here because it is so easy to forget it. We must give back to our people, white and colored, in this time of severe change, *something equal to or better than* that which has been taken away from them. We must not let people feel cheated, if it can possibly be helped, when great change takes place. When old defenses are torn down within an individual's personality without building up new defenses, that personality is likely to collapse into mental illness. When such change takes place in a culture, there will be great trouble unless we build up new defenses as the old go down.

Our South has been through one hard and terrible reconstruction. We do not want to go through another. And it will not be necessary—for our people have already demonstrated their capacity for change—*if we remember* that we must give our people new beliefs, new images of themselves to substitute for the old "superior white" and the old "hurt, frustrated Negro," new outlets for their frustrations, new and *creative* outlets. (I am assuming that segregation is going to be as hard psychically for many Negroes to give up as it is going to be for many whites.)

It is a tremendous responsibility, an awesome and fascinating job for our writers and speakers and teachers and leaders: to find new words for old; to create new images of ourselves without which we cannot live sane lives, to help men fall in love with new ideals, to find new outlets for the old hates and humiliations.

If we fail—we, the writers, the editors, the preachers and teachers—new, and perhaps far less wise leaders, will take our place. The vacuum will be filled. New words are going to be on the people's tongues. What these words are depends upon *us*.

* * * No writer in the South after the Civil War, except George Washington Cable, tried to give new images to our people. He gave us good words, but our people did not listen because only the one man spoke them. * * *

The poets, the wise men, the talented were mute. They withdrew to their ivory towers and let the political demagogues * * * take over the most precious task, the most important to the human being in time of change: that of giving him new, satisfying images of himself to live by, images created out of words.

What a sad and tragic thing this will be in our South if those who are gifted stay silent!

What words to use? What images to substitute for the old? While no writer or artist or speaker can tell others what to say, I think we can judge the rightness of our words, our feelings and acts, by checking and doublechecking them with the shape that the world's future is taking, and checking that future with man's old dream of himself as a unique and "sacred" and free person.

What is this shape? What is the new image of our world and of mankind that is growing in our imaginations?

Each of us has his own dream, each puts his own words to his dream. To me, this future holds no room for segregation in any of its forms, whether it be racial segregation, or banning of books and ideas, or political isolationism * * * or the split within men's own minds that isolate them from reality. The ancient patterns of withdrawal are the patterns of death and destruction.

Our new world will be a whole world; its people united under a democratic federation of nations; its unit will be the free individual, growing from childhood steadily toward a full maturity, accepting both freedom and responsibility, accepting all people as human beings with the same right to grow and to be different as he has. A whole world requires that whole men live in it. To have whole men means that we must have integrated individuals. To have integrated individuals means that our children must be given the chance to grow not as split-up personalities in whom body, mind, and emotions are forever warring, but as children kept whole, with strong creative loving egos that bind the body and personality together, and to their world.

Part of our fear today, part of the anxiety which so many feel, springs from the knowledge that this changing world requires that each of us change himself; that a world made whole means that each of us must be made whole, also. We want to be sure it is going to be worth it.

It seems worth it to me: to gain a whole new world for this split one that has warred with itself so long; to gain, in place of our old split-up personalities, health and stability. We are making a good bargain in swapping our old segregated world, our segregated southern culture, our segregated personality, for love and wholeness and dignity in men's relationships with each other and with themselves.

Therefore it seems to me a fine time to be alive, in this age of falling walls—the greatest age that mankind has ever experienced. It is an age full of risks but the stakes are high and worth the risk.

Ten years from today, I hope that I shall still be alive and I hope you will too, for it will be a fine thing to see this South of ours if each of us does our share in bringing these changes about *in a creative way.*

You young graduates have and deserve to have a sense of achievement today. You have completed four years of hard work, you have learned something, haven't you? A little? Maybe a great deal. You are ready to go out now and help make this new world of ours, knowing this time that the faith your fathers had and your older brothers had was justified, knowing that ten years from today those who come after you will never hide behind a wall again, that they will be strong human beings, standing on their own feet, doing their share to see to it that every human being on this earth has the two fundamental rights of mankind: the right to grow and the right to be different; knowing that these two rights make strong, unique individuals, and with strong, unique individuals democracy will be cherished and made to work across the whole earth.

THE RIGHT WAY IS NOT
A MODERATE WAY*

I want to take my stand by your side, tonight, because I respect the creative means you have chosen to use to secure your legal rights as American citizens.

These means are non-violent. This way is the way of good will and intelligence and truth, and love. You have refused to use the crude and dangerous weapon of hate. You have refused to lie. You have not succumbed to retaliation or to resentment. You have used no harshness of word or of act.

You have behaved under stress like mature men and women—not like a mob.

But you have not been "moderates" nor have you kept in the middle of the road. No. You have shown the world that there are two extremes and they cannot be put in the same moral category.

There is the extreme of hate, yes; but there is also the extreme of

---

* Speech sponsored by the Montgomery Improvement Association, read at the Institute on Non-Violence and Social Change, on the first anniversary of the bus boycott, December 5, 1956. Lillian Smith was unable to read the speech herself, due to illness.

love. There is the extreme of the lie; but there is also the extreme we call the "search for truth." There is the habitual thief who is certainly an extremist; but there is the habitually honest man who is an extremist, also.

Would you place the thief and the honest man in the same moral category? Would you put the person whose life radiates love in the same ethical category with the man whose life radiates hate? Are they equally harmful? Or equally good? Those who think so have abandoned the concept of morality and the concept of quality and sanity in human affairs.

So: You have been extremists: good, creative, loving extremists and I want to tell you I admire and respect you for it.

Moderation is the slogan of our times. But moderation never made a man or a nation great. Moderation never mastered ordeal or met a crisis successfully. Moderation never discovered anything; never invented anything; never dreamed a new dream. Moderation never wrote a poem, never built a skyscraper, never discovered a new drug, never made the first airplane, never painted a great picture, never wrote a great play, never explored a new frontier, never discovered new lands, never built a civilization, never dreamed a great religion. These great thrusts of the human imagination and spirit came out of daring to meet ordeal and need in a new way. It would be difficult to imagine Jesus as a "moderate." Difficult to imagine Leonardo da Vinci as a moderate. Imagine Gandhi as a moderate. Imagine Shakespeare or Einstein as a moderate. Imagine the young Lindbergh as a moderate: He may be one now but he was not one when he flew the Atlantic. It was the act of a daring extremist if there ever was such: but it was a creative act: not the act of a destroyer, nor the act of a hating man, nor the act of a violent man.

You have done many good things, down here in Montgomery. But one of the best, one of the most valuable, has been the fact that you have dramatized, for all America to see, that in times of ordeal, in times of crisis, only the extremist can meet the challenge. The question in crisis or ordeal is not: Are you going to be an extremist? The question is: What kind of extremist are you going to be?

Here, in Montgomery, you have decided what kind of extremist you are. You have chosen the way of love and truth, the way of non-violence and understanding, the way of patience with firmness, the way of dignity and calm persistence.

You have done this as others keep talking about moderation.

What do people mean when they use that fuzzy word, moderation? Why do the mass magazines keep talking about it? What makes the word so hypnotic? To answer that, we would have to write a history of the psychology of our times. But we can, at least, take a quick look at it:

In doing so, let us be as fair as we can. Many mean simply this: "We want to freeze things; we want to be neutral; we don't want to move a step either way. Things suit us as they are: why should we change them? Change is painful; so let's don't change." There are others, a few men of good will but with only a moderate amount of brains, who intend no harm at all when they lean back on this slogan. They mean in a vague way: "Let's be tactful; let's talk in a quiet voice; let's don't stir things up; let's try to sleep through it; then, maybe, someday we'll wake up and find that everything has settled itself." And there are a few sincere, even intelligent people who want moderation because the word, to them, means safety and security. They are too frightened to move or to think; too frightened to search for a new way to meet the challenge. It is known by all of us that our minds do not work well if we become too frightened, although they work best of all when we are a little frightened.

People behave this way in other crises, too; not simply in this one of race relations. There are people who react in a similar way when they are told they have cancer. They decide to be moderate and do nothing; to rock along and postpone thinking about it. Why? Because they are scared. And, because of their fright, they convince themselves that if they do nothing, if they take a few vitamins, maybe, the cancer will go away.

The tragic fact is, neither cancer nor segregation will go away while we close our eyes. Both are dangerous diseases that have to be handled quickly and skillfully because they spread, they metastasize throughout the organism. We have seen this happen, too often, to people who have delayed doing anything about cancer. We have also seen sick race relations metastasize throughout our country—and indeed, throughout the whole earth.

Because of the nature of both diseases—one physical, one social—because you cannot wall these problems in, you do not have time to lose with cancer; nor today, do we have time to lose in facing up to segregation, since the Supreme Court has spoken. The critical moment is on us. Now is the time to deal with it.

Why is there a crisis now? Why, after fifty years of segregation, has this way of life arrived at a critical turn?

As I see it, this is why:

The Supreme Court is the highest legal authority in our land. This Court interprets the U.S. Constitution for us. We are free men, yes; but we are not free in this country ruled by law, to interpret the law for ourselves, as Herman Talmadge says he does and claims that everybody can do. We have a freedom controlled by law; we do not live in a state of anarchy. Because this is true, when the Supreme Court speaks, we must obey. The Supreme Court has now spoken. It has said, segregation in the public schools must go because it is unconstitutional. The Supreme Court has said, in effect, that all legal segregation must go. Now: we are faced with a crisis.

But to say the Supreme Court's decision precipitated the crisis is only half a truth. It spoke its clear decision. The actual crisis came upon us because we did not listen. The ordeal became severe when the official leaders of our southern states spoke out defiantly and said they would not obey the Supreme Court's decision. After the Supreme Court spoke, it became irrelevant from the point of view of obedience to law, whether one did or did not want integration. The relevant matter was obedience to law. But these political leaders, many governors, many attorneys-general, many United States senators, defied the Supreme Court and began to try to force us to defy the Supreme Court (whether we wanted to or not). And in defying the highest law of our land and in compelling the citizens of certain states to do so, these politicians started a revolution against the legal structure on which our free and democratic government is based.

This is how the ordeal we are faced with, today, started. This is the situation we must now deal with: a very different situation from that of three years ago.

Three years ago, we had segregation. And it was the same old un-Christian, undemocratic way of life we had had for fifty years and have now; and people, colored and white, were harmed by it, as they are now being harmed. But the Supreme Court had not then challenged these old segregation statutes. Now: the situation is different. Different because legal segregation is against the law of our Nation. Different because, to maintain it, we must defy our own government.

How we deal with this critical situation, how we face up to it, will determine our moral health as individuals, our cultural health as a region, our political health as a nation; and our prestige as a leader of democratic forces throughout the world.

You know, as does everybody, how the destructive extremists are dealing with it in the South, and in the North. We are all aware of the mobs, of the Citizens Councils, of the Ku Klux Klans, of the quiet, stealthy injuries inflicted on those who want to obey their Nation's laws. But how are the rest of the white southerners dealing with it? May I trouble the waters, a little, by telling you?

A few white southerners—perhaps far more than you know—are dealing with it creatively and honestly and with courage. There are many white southerners opposed to segregation; there are millions who are not opposed to segregation but who believe it is more important to obey the law of the land than it is to have racial segregation. Some of these are speaking out: in the pulpits, in editorials. Others are meeting in small groups and probing deeply into this trouble in order to try to understand its roots. Others are taking, here and there, a bold stand. And some of these are losing their jobs, of course. But they think it is a small price to pay. They are the creative, non-violent "extremists" who are quietly, with wisdom and tact and good will, trying to bring change about as quickly as possible. They are attempting to meet ordeal with bold imagination, with skill and daring, but with sense and non-violence and sympathy for all concerned.

How about the others? The moderates? Those who are neither good extremists nor bad extremists? How about them?

Most of these so-called moderates are doing nothing. That does not mean they are not worried. It means they are suffering from temporary moral and psychic paralysis. They are working harder to be moderates than they are working to meet the crisis. They are driving straight down the middle of the road with their eyes shut and you know what happens in traffic when you do that. But they are trying to believe there is no traffic. They are telling themselves nobody is on the road but themselves. They are, you see, trying very hard not to be extremists: they are trying to be neither good nor evil.

And all the time these moderates are doing nothing or almost nothing, men like Herman Talmadge, men like Senator Eastland are shouting evil words at the top of their voices; and certain newspaper editors are writing violently against extremists—good and bad—and begging everybody to freeze and do nothing; and many of our mass magazines are belittling the good extremists and shouting that the "only way is the moderate way" . . . And as they beg the millions to be "moderate," the mobs gather, and the crosses are burned, and the houses are dynamited, and the brave ones who speak out lose their jobs and nobody cares much, and the few southern writers who speak out against segregation are penalized and nobody cares much, and young preachers lose their pulpits and nobody cares much; and so it goes, on and on . . . the White Citizens Councils mushroom, the Klan wakes up and wraps itself in pillow case and sheet—and Negroes and whites working for integration are threatened and penalized and cheated and confusion reigns.

But the big middle group turns away and tries not to see, whispering, "I must above all be moderate; I must not get worried; I must not mind when innocent people are hurt and brave people lose their jobs and lives. Some day it will settle itself, somehow."

And how are these moderates faring? What kind of price are they paying for their moderation, for this desire of theirs to keep things as they are?

It is a hidden price; it is not yet too obvious; but it is a high price. May I suggest what this price is?

In order to maintain the status quo, to maintain segregation as long as possible, even though the Supreme Court has spoken, in order to drive in the middle of the road, the white people of the South are giving up their freedoms. What freedoms?

Let me name a few:

a. The freedom to do right. * * *

b. The freedom to obey the law. * * *

c. The freedom to speak out, to write, to teach what one believes is true and just. We have almost lost this basic freedom now in the South. Teachers are compelled to sign statements that virtually strip them of their freedom to believe and to speak out. Penalties are imposed on those who speak out, anyway: jobs are lost.

d. And, having lost those three big freedoms, the precious ones that we Americans say we cherish, we are also losing our freedom from fear. In old Reconstruction days, white people were afraid of freed Negroes, or so they said. Today, they are afraid of each other and themselves. They fear. Front-door friends become back-door friends; some fear to be seen with a white southerner who wants to obey the law of our land. * * * And is this fear restricted to the South? Not at all: Magazines with mass circulation are timid about "offending the white segregationists." They fear, also. And this is very sad: to see our people, our proud, free people grow afraid to speak out and to act according to their conscience.

The risk is too big, people say. Young brave men say "the risk is too great. I'd like to do something but the risk is too big."

I say this:

> The time has now come when it is dangerous not to risk. We must take calculated risks in order to save our integrity, our moral nature, our lives, and all that is rich and creative in our culture. We must do what we do with love and dignity, with non-violence and wisdom, but we must do something big and imaginative and keep doing it until we master our ordeal.

I was talking, not long ago, to a group of students in one of our white southern universities. They had kind of sneaked me in. Yes, really. They were a little afraid for people to know Lillian Smith was on the campus. So everything was hush-hush. I teased them a little, because of its absurdity. And they laughed, and I laughed. But we all felt ashamed.

Not only the loss of our freedoms but the loss of our old gallant courage is part of the high price we are paying today for our do-nothing attitude toward segregation. For while the moderates are staying silent, the bad extremists are shouting at the top of their lungs. And because it is so difficult for the young white southerner to hear anything good and creative said, because he sees so little courage, so little valor among his elders, he is losing his beliefs in the good, creative, brave way of life. One young man said to me recently, "I'd risk anything for something I believed in. I just don't think I believe in anything much, anymore."

Then I told these young people about your creative project in Montgomery. They had heard a little, of course. But they listened, these young white men and girls, and they grew excited and interested and thrilled.

Do you, here in Montgomery, realize that in helping yourselves to secure your freedom you are helping young white southerners secure theirs, too? This is a big thing. This is how the creative act works: it always helps somebody else besides you.

In dramatizing that the extreme way can be the good way, the creative way, and that in times of ordeal it is the only way, you are helping the white South find its way, too. You are giving young white southerners hope. You are persuading some of them that there is something worth believing in and risking for. You are stirring their imaginations and their hearts—not simply because you are brave and running risks but because you know that the means we use are the important thing: the means must be right; the means must be full of truth and dignity and love and wisdom.

Because you are doing this, I want to close my greeting to you by saying, Thank you. Thank you for what you are doing for yourselves and what you are doing also for the entire South. Thank you for dramatizing before the eyes of America that the question is not, "Are you an extremist?" but "What kind of extremist are you?" Thank you for showing us all that there is always a creative, good, non-violent way to meet ordeal.

No Easy Way—Now[*]

May I tell you of my last visit to Arkansas? It was in the cold, bleak winter of 1940, after the mass eviction of sharecroppers from the plantations and farms. Do you remember? They were gathered on the roadside, hungry, homeless, cold, dismayed. A meeting to discuss their plight was being held in a small Negro church, near one of your small cities. It was snowing. A small wood-burning heater was red-hot but it did not, even so, heat more than a small circle around it. When you got too cold to endure it, you went up, warmed yourself, and went back to your chilly corner.

There were white people in that church, too. For always there have been in our South some whites who are concerned. I was there, observing; trying to understand what it was all about. There were, also present, the organizers from two competing unions. There, too, to help; but at the same time, a bitter power battle was going on between the two groups.

[*] Speech given for the Arkansas Council on Human Welfare, at the University of Arkansas, Fayetteville, October 23, 1957.

The room was filled with the misery of these bewildered, ignorant, worn-out, jobless human beings; but it was shot through with tensions of this competition. Things simmered down, finally; and the meeting was called to order. An old Negro preacher was asked to pray.

He stood up where he happened to be sitting. Just stood there: he put his rough old hands on the chair in front of him, and beat on it quietly. He was still, his hands grew still, and the room grew still. Then he prayed. This is what he said:

> Break their hearts, oh God. Give them tears.
> Tears . . .
> Make the tears flow, Lord; make them flow.
> Make a flood come.
> Wash away their hate, Lord; wash away their fears,
> Wash away them bosses, wash away their guns,
> Wash away them doodlum books,* wash away them po-lice, Lord.
> Wash away . . .

He prayed on: everything that had hurt his people he asked God to wash away, in the white folks' tears.

Today, as I return to Arkansas, I keep thinking of that prayer. I am not sure there is a better way to change things than for us to break our hearts and let the tears come. Perhaps only when our eyes are blind with tears can we see the new vision.

Our dilemma is complex; tangled; interwoven of many diverse threads. We are confused and we know it; we are frightened, and we know that, too. We feel not only rational fear but irrational anxiety: from the top-level of our reason to the bottom-level of our primitive

* "Doodlum books," was an expression used by sharecroppers to refer to the account books kept by the farmers for whom they worked, and used to substantiate the farmers' frequent claim at the end of the year that the sharecropper had increased, rather than lessened, his indebtedness to the commissary owner, and, hence, must remain as a sharecropper, on that farm, in a position of continued economic servitude.

mind we are stirred up and shaken and we are aware of it. We know the mob on the street is but a sign of the mob deep within our own minds, the disorder that tears at every heart.

And yet, this knowledge has not paralyzed us. We are searching for a way out: we are trying to find tactics or short-range goals to work for in this crisis; at the same time, we know that long-range goals are important and necessary. Part of our present confusion lies in this discussion about tactics and strategy, long-range objectives, short-range ones; it is quite obvious that even the most thoughtful among us are not agreed on which is more urgent.

Some think we should concentrate now on fundamental long-range goals: That we should pick up this problem of segregation, our so-called sacred way of life, and scrutinize it coldly and carefully; that we should ask a few sharp questions about it:

> What is so sacred about segregation?
> Why should we sacrifice law and order for it?
> Why should America risk the loss of the political
>   friendship of Asian and African nations because
>   of it?
> What has it done for our children? Has it made one
>   southern child, white or colored, a better person?
> Has it enriched our intellectual life?
> Is the segregated way of life economically profitable?

There are many fresh questions that can and should be asked about this system which the demagogues are demanding that we sacrifice so much for. And a few of our leaders feel we should concentrate *now* on these questions. They feel we must shake the minds of our people awake before real change can come to our region.

But others—and they are in the majority—believe we must, instead, concentrate on the short-range goals. These objectives can be summed up briefly in this way: We want our towns and cities

> to be free of mobs,
> to respect law and order,

to keep down agitators,
to curb the demagogues' influence,
to accept the Supreme Court's decision as law that
    must be obeyed whether we like it or not.

Looked at quietly, carefully, these seem to be minimal goals
which any sane, democratic, freedom-loving, God-fearing community could easily accept and easily achieve.

And yet: they have not been achieved. Nor even accepted as goals.

With a few shining exceptions, when crisis has come to the southern community the mob has come also; agitators have moved in; the
people have seemed indifferent to law and order; the demagogues
have put on their usual subversive act; the unwashed and illiterate
and criminal and psychotic elements have taken over our streets.
And we, who think we are free, strong, responsible, intelligent people suddenly realize we are dominated—not by a dictator, but by a
dictating idea which is embodied in a rabble so strong that the police
force and best leadership of the community are helpless to deal
with it.

Is this true? Is the rabble actually strong? No. Those who compose
it are few in number; they are weak in community influence, many
have criminal records, their intelligence quotients would run pretty
low: they are the riff-raff with no visible source of power at all.

Then where on earth do their power and strength come from?

To find it we must take two journeys:

The first one will be short. All we need do is walk over to Main
Street and enter a few modern air-conditioned offices. There, sitting
at their desks, are the men who quietly protect the rabble and give it
its hidden power. Some of these men are doctors, lawyers, bankers,
engineers, newspaper editors and publishers; some are powerful industrial leaders; most are known only in their hometowns and state
but others have important connections in New York City and Washington. They hold not only economic power but moral and civic
power, for they sit on church and education boards, on health
boards, on various local and state planning committees.

This is Mob # 2. It is a quiet, well-bred mob but far more dangerous than Mob # 1. Its members speak in cultivated voices, have courteous manners, some have university degrees, and a few wear Brooks Brothers suits. But they are a mob, nevertheless. For they not only protect the rabble on the street and tolerate its violence, they think in the same primitive mode, they share the same irrational anxieties of Mob # 1, and they are just as lawless in their own quiet way.

They don't dynamite houses and churches—they leave that to Mob # 1. They smother. By their use of boycott, threats, economic and [other] pressures they strip college professors, school teachers, preachers, writers, reporters, editors, students, their own employees, and many other white southerners of their constitutional rights to speak and write their beliefs and opinions. They also take away their right of peaceful assembly. These are precious rights to Americans. And a man who takes them away from a citizen is a law-breaker, just as much as the rough-neck who throws his weight around on the street.

Yet, because many people think only something *noisy* is violent, they are not aware of this insidious form of violence and lawlessness which is taking over our South and is creeping into the North, also.

Do these otherwise responsible, sensible men know why they play this shady role of protector of the street mob? Do they know why they strip their fellow-citizens of their lawful freedom of speech? Do we know? I am not sure that they or we understand their motivations.

But we need to find out why they are willing to risk so much for so little.

To find this answer, we must search for Mob # 3.

This will take us on a longer journey to the secret places inside our own personalities. Mob # 3 lives in the depths of our minds: It is activated by primitive fears, hatreds, guilts, some of which have nothing whatever to do with race. It is nourished on anxiety about the body image, on anxiety about our personal relationships, and on ancient myths of birth, death, blood, heredity, animals, darkness, and much else, of course.

Mob # 3 makes its home on the prehistoric, mythic level of the human mind. We are born possessing this symbolizing, word-making layer of mind—and everybody in the South seems to have an extra amount of it. It is a pity that reason is not also born in us. But we know, of course, that it is not: It is a talent, a skill, a method which has to be developed; we have the potentials, all right, for logical thinking but we are not born thinking logically. And unless we live in a culture which develops this skill in its people, [we] tend to have little of it.

It would be so much easier for us, when we are faced with crisis, were this mythic mind only a matter of emotions. We could then push it aside and say: Let's not feel; let's think it out; let's be realistic. But often when we assume we are realistic we are merely talking on a primitive level. The mythic mind has its *own mode of thinking* which is of a different nature from that of reason—and because it does think and talk in a different fashion, it easily tricks us.

When we reason, we look at facts; we evaluate them; check and doublecheck for accuracy; then we put fences around their significance. When we reason, we say, within this framework this concept is valid; outside the framework it loses much of its validity. Reason defines precisely; it tends to stave off generalization until it has collected enough facts and related them not only to each other but to a sufficient number of external situations to make the generalization stick. The chief characteristic of discursive logic is its tendency *always to relate its facts* to those in *the outside world*. (I hope you will forgive me for reminding you of what every one of us knows, when we stop to think about it.)

On the other hand, the primitive mind never relates: it merges. It is like a whale: it swallows everything in one awful gulp. It reaches out and pulls in the most disparate facts, feelings, situations, and concepts and squeezes them into one tight obsessive idea.

Its capacity for co-existence with inconsistency and irrelevance is unlimited. It takes the most diverse events and presses them into the same mold. A case in point is the facility with which Senator Talmadge, in a recent speech, stated that the marching-in of our American troops to Little Rock was of the same moral order as the Communists sending the Russian troops into Hungary. That ridiculous, false analogy came out of Mr. Talmadge's mythic mind and slipped immediately without criticism into millions of southern mythic minds, and quite a few northern ones, too, and it lies there, today, festering with resentment.

Above all else, the mythic mind is demi-urgic in its nature: It creates; it never criticizes itself or its own acts. Why should it? That is reason's job: to compare, measure, weigh, collect, test against past and present knowledge. Not so the mythic mind: It is impelled to make things, good and bad; to create things, good and bad. It can stir up a mob—or it can stir up a great symphony; it can scream lies and false analogies as our demagogues do (and a lot of other folks) or it can write a great poem, like Eliot's *Burnt Norton*. It can invent lethal weapons or dream up the great religions of the world.

But it does none of these good things, alone. Only when mated with reason and critical intelligence can the mythic mind become the fabulous creative imagination which invents, discovers, builds, writes, paints, dreams; only when it is impregnated with man's longing to be good, with his hunger for meaning, his need for a significant place in the universe can it dream of God—or dream of man himself growing in wisdom and awareness.

Without this mythic mind, we should be less than animals and far less than machines. For of course our power to symbolize comes out of it, and without symbols we could not even reason, and without symbolic forms there would be no art. Yet, when it is not controlled by self-criticism and reason and by the great ethical ideas so slowly thrust up through the centuries, it is the most dangerous thing on earth. We saw it working in Hitler and the Nazi party. We saw what happened when the potentially great creative forces in the German people, uncontrolled by self-criticism, uncontrolled by ethical ideas, and instead urged on by primitive myths of blood and sex and race made not great cities but concentration camps, devised not a good way of life but only a massive technic of murdering—and in the mad process pulled the whole world into a catastrophic war.

In the South, we long to be good; but we rarely tolerate criticism of our mistakes. We want to be Christian but we rarely permit our ministers to subject our way of life to the spiritual test of Christ's teachings. We long to be learned and we admire the physical sciences but we turn away from knowledge of our own minds and hearts and human relationships. We are not only afraid to talk about race we are afraid of all inquiry that comes close to man, himself. We are afraid of biology, psychology, psychiatry, afraid of all the social sciences. We are profoundly embarrassed when someone suggests that we look at the human condition. We turn away as if we have been shown a dirty picture.

Above all else, we are sensitive to criticism from our own fellow-southerners; so much so, that we try to punish them if they warn us that we are close to disaster. We southerners are endowed with a powerful and potentially creative imagination that could produce a rich culture and a great people. I believe that. But because we refuse to let it mate with critical intelligence and ethics, with poetry and mysticism, it tends to produce not strong, vital, free, creative individuals but sex-obsessed mobs; it thrusts up out of our soil not great leaders but irrational demagogues; it produces not healthy-minded, morally strong children but children confused and torn and weakened by learning to love ideals which they are commanded, even by state laws, not to love.

It is such a pity. It is more: it is our great tragedy. Like Medea we can cry: *I have done it: because I loathed you more than I loved them. Mine is the triumph. . . . I tore my own heart and laughed: I was tearing yours.*

Are all southerners like this? Are we all bereft of self-criticism? and blind? and complacent? Aren't some of us decent, sensitive, reasoning, honest, well-informed human beings who measure up well when compared to the best in our nation and world?

Of course. There are hundreds of thousands of southerners who do. But they are silent. They do not speak out. The question asked in this country and all over the world after Little Rock's trouble was: Why didn't the other ninety-nine thousand speak out? Why didn't the good, honest, intelligent people say something? A few did. But not enough; and perhaps the speaking came a bit too late.

Why don't we speak in time?

Because of fear of economic reprisals from Mob # 2, yes; and fear of physical violence from Mob # 1. But there is another reason: To speak against segregation is taboo; far more of a taboo than to break segregation by our acts. To understand this, once more we must look at that primitive layer of our minds: The *Word* is more powerful in the mythic mind than is the act. It is so, with small children, too; and in primitive tribes, the *Word* not only represents something, it *is* something; a magic something.

We were taught, in the South from early childhood, never to speak up against segregation. Now, when we do so, we feel anxious; we fear we may be wrong; our judgment may be bad; perhaps we shall hurt our families by this, we whisper; certainly we'll lose our usefulness. So we grow anxious; we become hysterically mute. Most of our moderation is nothing but mutism—as of course you know.

And we hug our secret beliefs to ourselves; we stubbornly teach them to our children and then let them know in devious, subtle ways that they cannot live them and must not say them aloud.

But secret beliefs do not create enlightened public opinion. And yet, only enlightened public opinion can stave off mobs and violence. The mob comes on the street when enlightened public opinion leaves it; the demagogues talk too much when the good, intelligent people talk too little. Mob thinking takes over only when reason and love and compassion have deserted our minds.

This brings us back to Mob # 2. Those quiet, college-bred men would not protect the street rabble if they did not believe they were morally supported by the rest of the responsible community. They would not use the boycott and economic reprisals in order to suppress all who differ from them, unless they felt their acts were approved. A few are evil opportunists who would do anything to build their power and increase their wealth. But not most of them. Most are confused men. They are just doing a lot of primitive thinking and feeling. And their consciences are almost clear: for their ministers, their newspaper editors, their friends in civic and business circles have not told them they are doing wrong. Almost nobody has told them, except perhaps their own wives, that segregation is not a sacred way of life.

It is easy to do wrong when everybody around you thinks you are doing right. It is difficult to take a stand all by yourself. It requires a whopping amount of moral courage—and more than most of us human beings possess. Especially in a region where at best, the intellectual deviant is looked upon as a crackpot and, at worst, as a perverse immoral half-insane creature.

We are, we must humbly confess, in the same pitiable condition of all brain-washed people. You don't have to live in a Communist country to be brain-washed. It can happen here at home; and has been happening to us southerners for nearly eighty years. We have heard on this subject of race—at least at home—only what the White Supremacists have told us. And there are too many people in other parts of our country who are brain-washed, also. They use the same old defenses, ask the same irrelevant questions, give the same mythic answers as we.

Even the president of the United States said in a recent speech on the Little Rock question that you can't "legislate morals." His variation was, I think, that "laws won't change men's minds." Now: who ever thought they would? Laws are to protect people—from those whose minds can't change; they are to protect people from the criminals who have no morals. But the implication of this statement (most popular among highly educated people) is: laws are ineffectual because they do not convert men. Yet what alternative is there to the rule of law save the rule of dictators? Unless we are willing to sink into anarchy and chaos. And which of these speakers about legislating morals would be willing to strike out our traffic laws, etc., etc.

Of course: When people speak like this, their mythic minds have taken over; their reason is sound asleep. Yet, these same men, on other subjects often speak with good sense and sometimes, extraordinary intelligence and wisdom.

This is what brain-washing does to a people. We talk like fools, in

Dixie and north of Dixie, too, about race and segregation; the Russians talk like fools about socialism and capitalistic imperialists, et cetera.

Are we not creeping now close to the heart of our trouble? Does it not center in two words: *fear* and *silence?*

We are acutely anxious, almost in panic, because silence has delivered us not only to the mob in the street but to the primitive, mob-like part of our own natures. And yet, we are so anxious that we dare not break the silence.

But: Were we to break it, we could quickly lift ourselves into the realm of reason and good feeling—just as we have done by our cancer drives which have substituted hope for anxiety.

We need a lot of real fear: the kind that looks at the actual dangers, and not at the imaginary ones: the kind that faces up to the danger that this racial turmoil will alienate new nations of Asia and Africa and throw them into the arms of communism. This is real: this concerns the survival of our nation, and the survival of democracy, and the survival of our way of life. We do have an American way of life that is great and good and worth sacrificing for—but it is not the segregated way the demagogues cherish.

But I refuse to blame all the trouble on the fear of our people. There are tens of thousands of brave southerners ready to speak out today—who don't have a place to speak. Ministers, whose boards won't let them; teachers who have had to sign pledges of silence in order to teach at all; editors who have been commanded by publisher and business manager not to write those editorials they dream of writing.

There are also hundreds of gifted, articulate white southerners ready to speak to the entire nation—and across the magnolia curtain of silence to their South—but where can they do it? Mass magazines don't want articles from white southerners who oppose segregation; they want articles from the "moderates" and from the separate-but-equalers—and from the Faulkners who say, "Give up, folks; there's nothing to do; whites and Negroes just don't like each other." (This is Mr. Faulkner's mythic mind speaking: the only mind he has ever shown evidence of possessing; for critical intelligence is not in his novels; only his mythic gift shows; it is great; it is wonderful; but it, alone, does not make great literature.)

How many of our informed white southerners who are opposed to segregation have you seen on TV and radio networks? I have appeared once for one fleeting moment—but who else? Yet, there are hundreds who are willing and ready. They simply haven't been asked. Yet Talmadge and Eastland and the Grand Kleagle of the KKK and the muted moderates have appeared numerous times. And a few thoughtful, courageous, sincere southerners who oppose mob rule and believe in obeying the law have appeared. But when asked how they felt about segregation, they did not take a stand against it. I do not questions their motives; I simply say the nation and the South have not heard white southerners speak up against segregation in mass magazines and on the networks—except in their superb news reports.

For some reason, and not necessarily an evil one, our friends in the North seem to have fallen for the White Citizens Councils' line: *Let Negroes speak, if they want to; let the Yankees speak; but don't let one intelligent white southerner who opposes segregation speak. Keep them smothered; only in this way can we sell the idea to the rest of the country that the South is unanimously opposed to the acceptance of Negroes as full-fledged American citizens.* *

This is the "line"—and the Councils have done an efficient job selling it at home and abroad. But it forms an impasse that somehow we must get around—or we cannot move far.

Here is where Mob # 2 has done its most iniquitous work. But remember: it has been able to do so only because Mob # 3, in the minds of millions of us, North and South, has given them moral permission.

Now: We are back where we began:

1. Should we work for short-range or long-range objectives?

---

* This had changed by 1965 [note appended by LS later].

2. Should we hush-hush the evil of segregation as it affects both whites and Negroes—and concentrate on keeping down mob rule and mob violence?

3. Should we postpone the job of educating our people regarding the evils and dangers of the segregated way itself—and instead sell the people the idea that laws must be obeyed whether we like them or not?

If only human beings were made in a simple, uncomplicated way, goal # 3 would be attainable. If only we could suppress their mythic minds and their critical minds at the same time. But of course, if we did, we'd have automatons and dehumanized slaves.

But we are human. And because we are, we always want to know real reasons, good reasons for a law. Our people will not obey a law which the demagogues and our own silence tell them is a silly, evil law. And we should not expect them to. We've all lost a lot of our rugged independence—but not that much. That "line" can be sold only to a people dominated by a dictator and the dictator has to do the selling. But our dictators down here in Dixie are not going to sell that line: that the change is inevitable and the law must be obeyed.

No. I am afraid we are going to do it the hard way or not do it at all: the hard way is the way man has always walked when he accepted the rigorous and the necessary:

1. By convincing our people that our actual survival as a nation depends upon this acceptance of Negroes as citizens;

2. By convincing them that this acceptance is not only necessary to survival but morally right, spiritually right for everybody concerned;

3. By working against mob rule, yes; but by realizing that the most dangerous mob we have is quietly existing on Main Street in some of our finest, most modern offices—not on the streets. We must tell our people so. They must realize where the power and strength of the street rabble comes from;

4. We are going to have to quell Mob #3 and we can do it only by showing the people how irrational is their fear of letting public barriers down between our groups of people. We can do it only by whistling that monster out of the caves of our minds—that Thing called Intermarriage—and show men and women how small and underfed it actually is. It is the smallest "danger" in our society, today.

We must do these hard jobs by encouraging the good people to break their silence: to take their stand for reason and criticial intelligence; for human dignity and human rights; for both the Negroes' public rights and everybody's private rights, stressing how both kinds of rights can be protected. * * *

But above all else, let's remember this: bad feelings are not chased away by reason: they are chased away by good compassionate feelings; hate does not die when it is repressed; it withers away only when it is replaced by love; anxiety is not driven out by silence but by voicing rational fear and by opening doors to hope.

There is no conflict between our short-range and long-range objectives. Both are necessary; both must be worked on simultaneously; not by the same person always; but both must be accepted as valid effort.

This is an all-out war we are involved in: a non-violent one but a war, just the same. Each must work according to his talent, his conviction, his place in society. But there is room for all of us who cherish freedom and the dignity of man and who use only non-violence in our work. What we are working against is evil, not men; never can we lose sight of that; always we must have compassion, magnanimity, and a good sense of humor around. It is very necessary.

And above all else, we must have hope, and courage; so much of it that we can face the ugliest aspects of the situation with equanimity: see it, appraise its strength—but keep searching for the good people, the ones willing to risk, the ones with tender hearts and tough minds.

We need to use the help of all who love their South and its people.

We need especially those who have shaken off the traumatic past, who face the future, and who know that neither our American future nor our world's future can be bought with those old Confederate bills, which the demagogues keep passing out to the people.

THE MORAL AND POLITICAL SIGNIFICANCE
OF THE STUDENTS' NON-VIOLENT PROTESTS*

I am going to talk tonight of the spiritual crisis which the South and its people are facing. We have been in ordeal a long time and have had outbursts of violence and localized crises again and again: in Little Rock, in Montgomery, Clinton, Nashville, Tallahassee, and in other spots in the South.

But what we are now facing is not localized and cannot be. It is something different, something that has not happened in this country before; it has a new quality of hope in it; and is, I believe, of tremendous moral and political significance. Somehow it is involving not only students but all of us, and there is a growing sense that what we say or fail to say, do or fail to do, will surely shape the events that lie ahead.

This hour of decision—and it is that for the South, certainly—was precipitated on February 1, by a Negro student, age eighteen, a freshman in a college in Greensboro, North Carolina. He had seen a documentary film on the life of Gandhi: he had heard about

* Speech given at All Souls Unitarian Church, Washington, D.C., April 21, 1960.

Montgomery and the non-violent protests made there; he had probably listened to Dr. Martin Luther King—certainly he knew about
him; he had his memories of childhood and its racial hurts: and he
had his hopes for the future. But millions of southerners, young and
old, and of both races, have had similar experiences. What else was
there in this young student that caused him to be capable of his
moment of truth? Courage, of course; and imagination, and intelligence—and enough love to respond to Gandhi's love of mankind, and enough truth-seeking in his mind to realize the meaning
of Gandhi's teaching of non-violence and compassion and their
redemptive and transforming power. Was this all the young man
had? No, there was more: an indefinable, unpredictable potential for
creating something new and lasting, and doing it at the right time.
Every leader and every hero, and many artists and scientists, possess
this talent for fusing their lives with the future. And yet, I doubt that
the young man knew he possessed this special quality, or even now
knows it.

In some strange way, however, his thoughts and memories and
hopes came together and he talked about what was on his mind with
three young friends. And a short time afterward, the four of them
went on their historic journey to a Greensboro ten-cent store.

From this small beginning, this almost absurd beginning, so in-
credibly simple and unpretentious that we Americans—used to the
power of big names and money and crowds and Madison Avenue
and Gallup polls—can scarcely believe in it, there started the non-
violent students' protests which have caught the imagination of millions of us.

Why are we stirred so deeply? What is it we feel? What are we
hoping for? I cannot answer for you. For me, it is as if the NO EXIT
sign is about to come down from our age; it is almost as if a door is
opening in a wall where there was no door. The older generations, to
which I belong, have found decisions so hard to make; they have
wobbled this way and that in their beliefs; they have postponed the
right action until the right time for it has passed. And now suddenly,
completely unexpectedly, the students' sit-in protests began, spread-

ing from college to college, school to school. It is exciting to watch them discover a freedom and purpose within themselves that they have not experienced in the outside world; to see them acting out, actually living, their beliefs in human dignity and democracy and in the redemptive power of love and non-violence, and going to jail for their beliefs.

* * *

Wait now, you say: You are giving these students quite a build-up. Do you actually think they are so extraordinary? No, I don't. I think they are probably quite ordinary young people in most ways: they are extraordinary only in their awareness that the hour we live in is an hour calling for courage and commitment, and they are making their commitment, and in doing so they are finding their courage. Actually, I suspect they were pretty shaky, those first ones who walked in the stores with their books and their Bibles to make their protest. They probably didn't have one grand, noble thought in their heads; they had made their decision in all earnestness and they were going through with it; and they were probably praying that they'd find the strength just to sit there; just sit there, that's all. But afterward, they must have felt an exaltation; a sudden rush of both pride and humility.

* * *

But even as I say this, I know the new life that is beginning, this spiritual renascence, can be snuffed out by you and me; by our apathy and stupidity and lack of imagination. I know police measures can become so cruel and massive and overwhelming that the students may not be able to take it. I am aware that a terrific effort will be made by certain powerful groups in the South who have close economic ties with the North to smother the movement by hushing the national press and the TV networks. I know that a few men in strategic places, by saying irresponsible things, as Mr. Truman did a few days ago, can throw pretty big obstacles in the students' path. There will be accusations of the most vicious kind, and misinterpretations, idiotic and dangerous, and there will be persistent persecution.

And it may be that these young students won't have the stamina to hold out. They may not find within themselves enough moral resources, enough psychic strength to carry them through the bitter and bleak days ahead of them. I know, too, that the white students of the South may not be able to break out of their apathy and moral paralysis in large enough numbers to help the young Negroes in this struggle for a new life, and without help the burdens may prove too heavy.

But I believe the movement *can succeed* if enough of us have the imagination to see its significance and its creative possibilities and to interpret these to others who do not see; and if we give the students the moral support and the money they are going to need. There is a tremendous power in the non-violent protest that the sensitive southern conscience and heart will find hard to resist; but even so, the students may have to struggle a long time. They will need friends during their ordeal. Americans in other sections can help them and should, for this not only concerns the South, it concerns the entire nation and the nation's relationships with the rest of the world. It also concerns each person's relationship with himself and his beliefs.

But there are some things that only the South can do. Things that only good, responsible, decent southerners can accomplish. Only they can create a new climate of opinion in which mob violence and the hoodlums and the police and the White Citizens Councils can be controlled; and they can do this only by breaking their silence and speaking out. To speak out for law and order is not enough, today; there is a higher law which we southerners must take a stand on, that concerns justice and mercy and compassion and freedom of the spirit and mind. Thousands of us must also speak out against segregation as a way of life; not simply racial segregation but every form of estrangement that splits man and his world into fragments. The time has come when we must face the fact that only by speaking out our real beliefs, and then acting on them, can we avoid a bitter time of hate and violence and suffering.

But will the southerners do it? I don't know. I hope so but I do not know. They let Little Rock happen when they could have kept that debacle out of the history books simply by taking a stand for the right things. They are now, in Birmingham, letting even worse things happen.

Our responsible people's silence is not because they are in the minority: they outnumber the demagogues and Klans and hoodlums and crackpots twenty to one. In their hands are the media of communication: the pulpits, the TV and radio stations, the newspapers. They have the power and the money, the education and the technics to create an atmosphere of vigorous, healthy-minded concern wherein good words can be heard and the good act carried through; an atmosphere where people can plan, think clearly, and find ways to do what is right.

Why, then, are they silent? Why do they evade their responsibility at this time of crisis?

Is it fear? I don't think so. I think it is anxiety. There is a vast difference between the two.

It is difficult to analyze a complex state of mind in just a few minutes but let me try: We white people of the South think of ourselves as free but we are chained to taboos, to superstitions; tied to a mythic past that never existed; weakened by memories and beliefs that are in passionate conflict with each other.

The tragedy of the South lies just here: segregation has made psychic and moral slaves of so many of us. We think we are a free people but we have lost our freedom to question, to learn, to do what our conscience tells us is right, to criticize ourselves. We are torn apart inside by a conflict that never lets up, and we wall our minds off into segregated compartments. How can a man believe simultaneously in brotherhood and racial discrimination? In human freedom and forced segregation? How can he fight Communist dictatorship and surrender himself to the dictatorship of an idea like White Supremacy? How can he do and think these things and fail to see the moral inconsistency, the intellectual absurdity of his position?

But many southerners can. And some of them are educated men who think of themselves as the community's moral and civic leaders.

The psychic result has been that a deep anxiety possesses them and they feel that any change would be only for the worse. When they are asked why they fear the crumbling of segregation they cannot tell you that what they really fear is the crumbling of the walls inside themselves. Instead, they talk about intermarriage. It makes poor sense but they think it explains their acute anxiety.

But there are other southerners who have changed, who don't like discrimination, who don't believe in segregation. And I am often asked, Why don't they say so? Some are speaking out, of course; hundreds of them; others want to but are afraid they will do "more harm than good." Here, once again, we have the result of a rigid, inflexible training in early childhood, given to us during a time of panic and dread. I was born at the turn of the century when the first segregation statutes were being put on the law books of the southern states. During the first ten years of my life there were almost a thousand lynchings in the South. It was in this atmosphere of terror and brutality, of internal and external disorder, that we were taught our lessons in segregation. No wonder so many southerners of my age cling to it. We were told as children never to question it, never to talk about it. This silence that is today so dangerous to us and so puzzling to others is a built-in silence; its foundations go down to babyhood; to our mother's hushed whispering; there is a hypnotic quality about such learning and only the rebellious mind, the critical intelligence, or the loving heart can defy it.

The truth is that our parents and grandparents paid a terrible price for a security which they believed segregation could give them. When they permitted the system to be set up, they did not foresee that emergency measures would be frozen permanently into state laws. They did not dream that segregation would become a ritual so sacred that it would be given priority over the teachings of Christ in our churches. They did not know a time was ahead when the politician would exert more influence than the preacher. The history of the political and social and psychological pressures that caused our fathers to blunder in so tragic a way is too complex to go into here. Let us settle for this: that the price they paid for security was exorbitant and their white children are still paying today. For they have been as surely injured in mind and spirit by segregation as have Negro children: both have been warped, both have been kept from a free, creative life; both find it difficult to be courageous, strong individuals who can defy conformity and find their own responses to the world.

But some white southerners are speaking out; and more would if they could hear others do so. There is a serious lack of communication between liberal southerners. We can't hear each other speak because there are so few places where the person who opposes segregation can speak in the South. The local radio and TV forums have not as yet been opened up to many white southerners who oppose segregation; nor have the national forums been opened to them. Again and again, on TV, the nation sees Senator Talmadge and Senator Eastland and other racial demagogues and hears them say the same old things they've said for years about mongrelization. Why can't we have a change? There are eloquent and courageous young ministers in the South who oppose segregation, and have something fresh to tell the country. To hear them on networks would give encouragement to those in the South who have never heard any southerner state in a public speech that he is opposed to segregation. This is one way to help break the taboo of silence.

Once the silence is broken the South will change quickly. More quickly than we think. There are so many ready for change: thousands of ministers who have taken a good stand; hundreds who preach strong eloquent sermons against segregation; there are close to a hundred thousand women in Georgia alone, who are willing to give up segregation in public places including the schools; and there are hundreds of them working hard every day to rid our state of a system that has hurt everybody. These women are informed; they have thought and studied and examined their own souls, many of them, and have given their children better training in human relations—certainly in terms of race—than my generation had.

It is important for us to break the word "South" into a thousand pieces: not only geographically, but economically; not only culturally but in terms of the sexes, not only vocationally, not only psychologically; but also into generations: there are gradations of opinion in all of these groups, and gradations of moral strength. What is terrifying to the older generation (those born when segregation was being set up in the South) doesn't bother the young students; the southerner over forty is likely to suffer from taboos the eighteen-year-old does not feel; what paralyzes the men often releases the women; what seems easy to do for the twenty-five-year-old seems impossible to the fifty-year-old; the poor and ignorant often feel a psychic and social hunger to belong "to the white race" as if it were a club, while the more sophisticated, the more secure economically and culturally do not have this need; their sense of "belonging" has come to them in other ways. In certain areas of work, there is no racial competition; in others the competition is severe and exacerbates race feelings. And too, differences go beyond the groups; the South is chock-full of individuals each with his own ideas—this, despite our somewhat totalitarian training and our one-party political system. People may act the same under pressures and not feel the same or believe the same or have the same values. (This may be as true of Russia as it is of the South.) The false lumping of all southerners together by those who speak and write of us is not a good thing and makes for identifications which we don't feel, or accept.

*　*　*

These differences among our people are potentially good; this lack of conformity in feelings and beliefs keeps the door cracked. What we need to know is that these differences exist. We need to know that millions of people are no longer for segregation. That is why I have such hopes for the students' non-violent protests. They are encouraging responsible people to speak out. If white students will join in large numbers with Negro students, their experiences of suffering together, their self-imposed discipline and philosophical training will create a fine reservoir of new leadership for the South. We cannot change the South until we change our leadership, and we cannot change leaders until we change ourselves. We, as a region, can have our moment of truth only when we begin to think of ourselves not as members of races but as persons; we can take the walls down outside only by taking the walls down within us. Then it will come. And it will be a healing time for us, and perhaps the whole world, for we are so sensitized to one another, so closely related by the common purpose of creating a future, that whatever brings wholeness to us will bring wholeness to millions of others across the world.

Perhaps, even now, our moment of truth is near; let's pray that it does not turn into an agonizing time of sin and error.

Acceptance Speech for the
Charles S. Johnson Award

I am sorry that I cannot be with you. My old enemy cancer is now battling me hard—so I speak to you from my bed.

I am deeply grateful to be given the Charles S. Johnson Award for I knew him well and loved and admired him.

Dr. Johnson knew that we live in a world that is round. And he rejoiced in it, as did that great scientist and prophet, Teilhard de Chardin—knowing it to be the simplest and most complete statement that can be made about human destiny.

Because our earth is round we cannot escape each other; century by century we are driven closer together. This proximity has had a miraculous effect: it has produced human culture: something man himself has created. For a half-million years of his own creation man has lifted himself to what he is; by means of a beautiful interlocking of facts and discoveries, dreams and words, visions and love he has become *Man*. But man is young, compared with the ants he is a baby; most of his evolution of spirit and mind lies ahead of him. It is as if God has said: "The rest is now up to you." God is not dead— God has apparently decided it is time for man to grow up, to participate [more fully] in his own evolution.

So: we are faced not by a future without purpose, but a future *with* a purpose so challenging, so exciting that we dare not accept it all at once.

We are just beginning to see that the age of ideologies is over and we are entering the new age of human relations. It is *his millions of relationships* that will give man his humanity. And we are now at the open door of this new age.

It is not our ideological rights that are [now most] important but the quality of our relationships with each other, with all men, with knowledge and art and God that count.

The civil rights movement has done a magnificent job but it is now faced with the ancient choice between good and evil, between love for all men and lust for a group's power. It must choose between racial ideology and human relations. Every group on earth that has put ideology before human relations has failed; always disaster and bitterness and bloodshed have come. This movement, too, may fail. If it does, it will be because it aroused in men more hate than love, more concern for [their] own group than for all people, more lust for power than compassion for human need.

What I have tried to do during these many years has been to give vision, to open up a wider path towards man's future; I have tried to arouse hope that the future holds a wondrous challenge for our children. It is not something to dread. It is something to prepare for by increasing our knowledge, polishing our intelligence, cultivating our love and compassion and humor and patience and fortitude and courage.

We must avoid the trap of totalism which lures a man into thinking there is only one way, one answer, one option, and that others must be forced into this One Way, and forced into it *Now*.

Segregation is evil; there is no pattern of life that can dehumanize men as can the way of segregation.

But "integration" (a meaningless word in terms of one man's relation with another) may or may not be the right answer at a given time. Integration rhymes with segregation but that is about all it has to do with it. Segregation must go; it must not be permitted in our communal life; but so-called integration may not be the best and only answer as we search for ways of relating ourselves to one another; as we search for unity, while still maintaining diversity, as we search for means of collaborating *as human beings for human ends.*

This search is the big job of our age: a purpose we should commit ourselves to, whether we are artists or scientists or technicians or teachers or religious leaders. As one writer I have tried, only to work toward this end.

II

WORDS THAT CHAIN US AND WORDS THAT SET US FREE

The essays and speeches which make up Part II of this collection describe issues greater in scope than the political and social struggle of the American South. In many of these writings, segregation and racism are points of departure for discussions of varied and far-reaching concepts. Among these are: the power of language; the proper—i.e., moral—use of language; the political responsibility of the creative person; the "human condition" of existence in an unexplained, infinite cosmos, which is the primal segregation of humanity; the postwar "human condition" of existence under the potential of nuclear war and in a shrinking world; the mythic mind and its power to create and manipulate symbols; the necessity for difference, and of a respect for difference, in humans. Some of these ideas are contained in the writings in Part I, in Part II they are more fully developed.

Part II opens with an excerpt from a speech given at a rally in Washington, D.C., July 21, 1951. This is followed by "The Winner Names the Age," a commencement address at Atlanta University on June 3, 1957, which explores the historical reality that it is the "winners" of an age (those whose influence and ideas survive into the new era) who characterize that age for all time. In this speech, Lillian Smith lists what she considers the three most powerful factors in the postwar world: the remarkable advances in communication; the control of atomic energy; the presence of 2.5 billion free people. In order to realize the potential for good of these factors, the citizens of this smaller, more powerful, and freer world must be individuals who will not give over power to demagogues, thereby allowing demagogues to name the age.

"A Trembling Earth," a speech requested by Paris radio in the late fifties, comments on Smith's own novelistic descriptions of southern life, and on the descriptions of other southern writers: Faulkner, Wright, McCullers, Williams, Ellison. One of the main points of the speech—repeated by Smith in "Out of Creative Tensions Will Come Peace" and "The Role of the Poet in the World of Demagogues"—is that the writer must seek to describe a view which is not limited, and which takes, boldly and courageously, responsibility for the "agony and dreams and the potentialities of modern man in a modern nightmare world."

"Out of New Creative Tensions Will Come Peace," an article published in the *Saturday Review* in 1960, asks the question, "have we lost our commitment to the future?" Smith asserts that the primary problem in the modern world is not war, nor the threat of war (we must remind ourselves that she was writing this during the height of the fallout shelter/nuclear war panic) but the "dehumanization of man." She uses segregation as a symbol of the "estrangement" of modern humanity: "the loss of communication with our own self." Smith sees the redefinition of human life and human values as an absolute necessity if we are to survive.

"The Mob and the Ghost," a talk given at Emory University, April 27, 1961, opens with a description of the intricate system of lies, half-truths, and hypocrisies with which Lillian Smith was faced as a child in the racist South. She speaks of the chasms which stood between her and real knowledge—the knowledge, on the one hand, of the racism of those she was taught to respect and love, and the search for the answers to those "existential" questions which haunted her. In these essays and speeches she reiterates these questions, observing that the institution of segregation is in a sense an escape route for humans from the innate terror of life in an undefined universe.

This speech, and the essay which follows—"Words That Chain Us and Words That Set Us Free," an article in *New South* (March 1962)—analyze an incident which occurred in Athens, Georgia, in January 1961. Charlayne Hunter, the first female black student to enter the University of Georgia, was attacked one night by 2,000 students armed with rocks, who stoned her dormitory window. This incident defined the level of fear and confusion—the mob-thinking—of southern whites vis-à-vis blacks. Smith uses this incident to demonstrate the danger of believing in symbols or "ghosts" in real situations. The students armed with rocks, she observes, were aware only of what they had been led to believe about blacks and whites, and also women, and perceived Charlayne Hunter not as an individual, a real person, but only as a symbol of the overthrow of these beliefs.

"Words That Chain Us and Words That Set Us Free" also includes Smith's argument that equality is a false standard which in fact serves the demagogues of segregation. She correctly states that equality is impossible since no two human beings are the same. Equality is a viable concept only as it relates to a person's civil rights. Perhaps the most important point in this essay is Smith's assertion of the "right to be different." This is a right central to the struggle of any group: religious, racial, ethnic, sexual. Conformity, sameness are not standards to be followed, to be struggled for—it is difference, Smith asserts, that we must claim as our natural right.

The final essay in this section is "The Role of the Poet in a World of Demagogues," prepared as an acceptance speech for the first Queen Esther Scroll presented to Lillian Smith by the Women's Division of the American Jewish Congress on March 17, 1965. Smith speaks here, as elsewhere, about the power of language to change political and social situations; and of the role of the creative person to seize the opportunity to do this.

DREAMS AND REALITY*

Dreams and reality . . . One often hears people say "I am a realist." And they say it, usually, with a little sneer at idealists. Now the idealists are the dreamers of the world and if they are real idealists they make their dream come true. They deal with the future; they create our future. The so-called realist is concerned with the past. He is concerned with something that is finished, that has already been made, already created.

Dreams and reality . . . There is no conflict between those two words. One is only the beginning of the other. The dreamer dreams, he falls in love with his dream, he talks about it until others fall in love with the dream and then together they make it into reality. Whenever you hear a person sneer a little at an idealist and say "Now I am a realist," watch out. For he is a phony realist, not an honest one. An honest realist is one who helps make a dream into reality. One cannot do that unless one is both a dreamer and a doer. A man who acts without dreaming is exploiting somebody else's dream. I

* Excerpted from a speech given at a rally in Washington, D.C., July 21, 1951.

think you can count on that being true. He is turned toward the past not the future.

We, here today, have our face to the future. It is a good future, I think, and we can launch out into our job with confidence, knowing that we are in step with this good future. We are working to make it possible to grow whole children who can keep their world whole.

THE WINNER NAMES THE AGE*

Well, it is over now, isn't it? The easy part: the research, the thesis, the long hours in the library, the field work. In a sense, it was so safe and secure, hard but pleasant, this learning process; this easy, cloistered way of life when one makes a friend or two, grows a bit in mind and heart and imagination, and picks up so many useful and useless facts.

All this you have done in the front rooms of your mind.

But in the back room, somewhere inside you, in a secret corner, you have been painting a picture: a picture you began when you were a child, long before you knew words. You have not named that picture yet; perhaps you never will; we usually don't. Although most of us call it names—and I'm sure you, too, in your nasty moods, have plastered it with insults. But you have not decided, yet, what to name it.

For it is a picture of you; of your dreams and feelings, your sudden vision, your awareness, your hopes and despairs, a picture of all that

---

* Commencement address at Atlanta University, June 3, 1957.

this fabulous human experience has meant to you up to now—or failed to mean.

What your style is, I don't know. That is your secret. All I know is, that style is patterned on *you*: on *your unique way* of looking at your world. It may be gay and bold and strong in its brushwork, compassionate in its feeling, or it may be as full of terror and angry protest as Picasso's *Guernica*. You may have painted an abstraction; it may be non-objective; it may be blobs and dots, dribbles and improvisations, with, maybe, the bright colors, the startling accidents of a Pollock; or you may be slowly finding its form, and even now, it may be taking on a little of the strength and equilibrium of—shall we agree on a Cezanne? Or if you dare not look beneath the surface of life, or above it, it is probably as literal as an amateur photograph.

But whatever it is, it is your picture of the human experience and *you* have painted it. And when you leave the campus, that picture will go with you, along with the facts and the theories, the methods, and all the rest of it you have learned here.

And you will keep on painting it. You may lay aside one canvas and start another but you'll keep at it, searching for a quality of truth that eludes you. Searching for the underside of meaning; searching for its poetry, its music, and its pain. Or maybe you won't. As the years go by, you may decide its colors are too harsh, its lines too broken, too jagged, and you may do that cruel thing: touch it up a little. You may finally say, I cannot bear the truth, even the small image of it I have made: I'll make it softer, prettier—and less true. I'll paint life as a paper doll, or a marshmallow. A lot of us do that, too, you know.

Whatever you do to it, that image of your universe, of you and your experience of life, is *yours*. I could not change it if I wanted to. And I shall not try.

What I want to show you is something else. Not my picture of my experience of life: if you want to see a smidge of that, you can read my books. What I want us to look at together, now, is a kind of rough, crude blueprint of this age of ours: of the common ordeals—full of danger and opportunities which we, regardless of private views or personal interests, must face together.

It is an age that has no name. Nor will it soon have one. It has often been called "the Age of Anxiety," but it will not, I think, be known in history as that. For the winners would not call it so: and the winners do the naming.

Sometimes we forget this. We forget that always an age is named for its triumphs, always for the big ideas that add stature to the human being. A brief glance at any great age, but let's make it the eighteenth century, will remind us how true this is. We call that century the Age of Reason, of Enlightenment, of the Rights of Man. And that is the way we think, today, of those troubled, terrible times. For the ideas of that century, the symbols that stirred the Western mind so deeply, the daring acts, were the winners who named the baby.

And yet, actually, the Age of Enlightenment was an age when most Western men could not read or write. The Age of the Rights of Man was a time when a new slavery was sending deep roots into American soil, and a new colonialism was beginning to lay its greedy paws on Asia and Africa.

Let me remind you of a few other things that were happening in this great Age of Reason. It was a time when educated Europeans were deeply concerned about ghosts. The Oxford University magazines were full of discussions of ghosts. Samuel Johnson took part, as you might know he would have, in this controversy—widespread in England. Witches, too, were still a hot topic. This Age of Reason was an age when the blind and crippled were persecuted and half starved; when the mentally ill were chained and some were whipped to death; when epileptics were hidden away; when men looked on tuberculosis and cancer as punishments from God.

This great intellectual era that gave us Rousseau's and Locke's writings, Voltaire's bold, sharp, ironic questions, Thomas Paine's books, and Jefferson's words on liberty and human freedom, gave us also a curious best-seller which swept Europe like wildfire. It was translated into English, French, and German and was read by the intelligentsia. Parents were deeply impressed by it and shaped their methods of child guidance on it; clergymen preached on the morality it implied; doctors based their therapies on it and continued to do

so, some of them, until the twentieth century. You may not, perhaps, have heard that book's name: It was called *L'Onanisme* and
was written by a physician named Tissot. And it was concerned with
the secret "sins" that children commit. According to this expert those
sins caused most of the diseases known to man: from fits to diarrhea,
from insanity to blindness, deafness, muteness, cerebral palsy, rheu-
matism, anemia, liver upsets, and the like.

This, all this, came out of the great Age of Reason.

Even so, even though the eighteenth century was chock-full of
hysteria and superstition and irrationality we are right to call it the
Age of Enlightenment. For the germinal ideas it brought to life, the
vision of man's possibilities which is communicated to the future in
impassioned words and symbolic acts, will never die. They are,
today, a part of the human heritage. And will remain so as long as
men live on this earth.

There is always a dark underside to every age, a festering ill-smell-
ing slum where man's enemies and errors breed. But an age is remembered not for its enemies and errors but for those qualities it
dramatized which enlarge horizons and give a fine ambience to man,
himself. Malraux was right when he said, "Always, however bru-
tal an age may actually have been, its style transmits its music only."

You and I can paint our picture but we cannot name our age; the
winner will do that. What we *can* do is pick the winner.

And because we can, I would like for us to take a look at the conditions, the ordeals out of which the winning ideas, the triumphant attitudes and technics will come.

We are faced with three which men have never had to deal with
before. Each holds high potentials for good and evil, for life and
death. Each affects the others. All three are concerned with new
forms of power. And all will shape the earth's future.

You are as familiar with them as I am. But let us tie them a bit
more tightly together; weigh their dangers in a lump and see what we
can make of it.

The first can be described quite simply: It is the new power of
world opinion. Walls are down. Distance has been obliterated.

Communication lines, economic and political lines are strung everywhere, each crisscrossing the others, with the result that there is no longer a place for secrets. We cannot, as nations, gossip about each other without being heard. We cannot trick each other without being found out. We cannot hold, for ourselves, alone, either new things made or new knowledge gained. We can try but world opinion is powerful and will have its say about it.

This is a totally new thing: this publicity, this tied-togetherness, and this capacity for quick reaction. Suddenly the earth is stripped of its old insulated silence, its slow come-back, and is transformed into a sensitive instrument which responds with electronic speed to whatever is said and done. A few tactless words spoken by an official of one country can upset the government or economy of another. One stupid act, today, can bring on a world crisis, tomorrow. Even the blunders and crimes of individuals can make foreign offices tremble.

It is obvious that we have not yet developed an earth-sized courtesy and tact; nor have we yet found the new concern and new morality, and new objectivity, to match the new publicity and the new intimacy. Until we do, this new power of world opinion will oscillate between good and evil, life and death. It will be on somebody's side, yes; but not necessarily on the right side.

Our second ordeal is in everybody's mind: *Atomic energy and how to control it*. We know that nuclear power has fabulous possibilities for good; we know it can become a great creative force in the future, but what troubles people everywhere is its danger to us *right now*.

We are anxious and concerned: not only because the bombs can bring quick and total destruction in war, but because peacetime testing of bombs has already brought unknown damage to the human race. We are concerned that radioactive fall-out causes an increase in cancer in children. We are concerned that the fall-out has already affected the genes of a percentage of our young people everywhere. What percentage? We are not sure. How many of their children will be defective and malformed? We do not yet know. But we want to know.

A few scientists have spoken clearly. We want more of them to speak, and in more detail. And we do not want the politicians to brush off these words. For the scientists are the only men on earth who know what they are talking about when they state the facts about radiation and its effect on the human race. We are afraid of politicians and atomic committees who try to keep secret the scientists' warnings. We are afraid of those stubborn men who continue the testing, in spite of the advice of some of the world's greatest authorities. This is where world opinion can play its first great role in history. It, alone, can compel governments to use nuclear energy in the right way. If it wants to, it can measure its strength against the atom, and it can win. But will it? That is our decision.

Our third ordeal is living in a world with two and a half billion free people. This is a new thing: it can be a wonderful thing, a fabulous time of greatness can come out of it, but it is also dangerous: because *free people have power*—more power than a half-dozen H-bombs.

They are not likely to blow up the earth with their power but in their ignorance and inexperience, they may blow up civilization. They can destroy art and music and poetry and books and criticism; they can tear up laboratories and libraries; they can jail scientists and intellectuals and artists; they already decide what can be shown on TV and in the movies; they already dictate to the mass magazines; they can even dynamite churches (as we in the South well know). They can, *when out of control*, do all these terrifying things because *freedom gives them strength*. A free man with the vote, and with wages that give him purchasing power, is armed with some hefty weapons.

This problem of free people and their new and amazing power does not disturb Communist countries—not as long as they have a strong secret police. Dictators keep the people under control by taking away their freedom, by working them hard, starving them half to death, terrorizing them if they protest, and killing them when necessary.

No, it is the democracies that feel this power. Democracies—and remember, we are trying to turn the whole world into democracies—cannot have uncontrolled free people around. They cannot have this much power on the loose. Controls are necessary. But controls must be democratic, they must function without taking away the essential civil liberties of all men. What are the controls that are valid and will work?

A powerful control is constitutional law. A democracy can't do without it. But it will work only if the people believe in law and respect its processes.

But the two strongest and best controls come from within a free man's own mind: his conscience and his reason. Both of which—to stay healthy—must be nourished on civilization's great and germinal ideas. May I name a few? Just to hear the music of them? for they sing to the civilized mind:

> the idea that every child has a right to grow;
>
> the idea that every one in the community has a right to be protected from violence;
>
> the idea that all people can speak out and say what they think;
>
> the idea that a man has a right to be different in looks, beliefs, interests, and talents if he does not injure others;
>
> the idea that truth is a search that must never stop, that both reason and imagination are necessary to that search, that the scientific method is necessary, too, and cannot be interfered with except when human life is jeopardized or profound human values cheapened;
>
> the idea that the way a thing is done, the means used, are as important as the end sought;
>
> the basic idea: that God is the Ultimate Concern beyond all men, that He is the supreme symbol: not the white race, not the Communist party, not capitalism, not any authoritarian group; and that his laws of love and brotherhood and mercy and compassion must be obeyed.

When men stop believing in these great ideas, when they silence their conscience and trample their reason, when they make their own image their god—or their economic or political beliefs their god—then we are in for trouble. For then, they hold even constitutional law cheap. They sneer at the high courts of their government; indeed, they say they obey only the laws they want to.

When this happens, the free people with their limitless potentials for growth and for good will metamorphose into the mob.

* * *

Here is the crux of the matter: In a democracy, enlightened, civilized public opinion must prevail; not mob opinion, but the opinion of millions of individuals who have held on to their reason and conscience, and their belief in the free, growing human being.

The only way this public opinion can prevail is for people to stand up and speak out. Those who believe violence is wrong must say so. Those who believe a man has a right to be different must say so; those who believe a clergyman should preach according to his religious conscience should say so; those who believe school-teachers must not be asked to take a loyalty oath defending segregation or the "southern way of life" or capitalism or any other form of idolatry, must say so; those who believe that our artists and writers must be left free to create their dreams and ideas into paintings and books must say so. Those who believe survival is more important than security must say this, too. For otherwise democracy cannot survive, nor, I think, can civilization survive. For the mob's power can destroy our freedom as completely as can any Communist dictator.

What a price we have paid for silence! So many decent, warm-hearted, intelligent people are silent today—not only in our South but all over our country, surrendering their opinion because they are torn between the teachings of their childhood and what they, today, know in their minds is right; or silent because they are afraid to make the hard and necessary choice.

In their efforts to be moderate or neutral, they either do nothing or something totally irrelevant to the situation. And in a crisis that is a dangerous kind of behavior.

The power of free people has to be controlled, channeled, disciplined by values and knowledge, and law—or it can be more dangerous to us than hysterical world opinion (which it is close to) or than nuclear energy, out of control.

Because this is true, I consider the demagogue the greatest enemy a democracy has. Not the dictator: that is Communism's problem. Our problem is the demagogue: the man who deliberately betrays the people; the man who scares them, calling fire when there is no fire; who tells the people they are free to break the law, free to trample other people's rights, free to slough off their conscience and their reason and behave like madmen when they want to. This is the number one subversive man in our culture; this man is the people's real enemy. For he deliberately breaks down the controls of the church, of conscience, of civilization, of the courts, to get the people under his control.

What can we do about it? Ah, how everyone whispers this to himself, his family, his close friends!

The answer lies first in leadership; second, in the determined efforts of each individual to take his stand, to speak up, and try to create a climate of courage and hope and faith. Without the second, we cannot have the first. We need leaders, not martyrs. But we cannot have leaders unless the best people stand by the leaders, unless we give support when support is needed.

For fifty years, the South has had no great leader from the white race. Demagogues by the bushel but not one great leader. This, too, is part of the price we have paid for our silence and for walling ourselves away from the great ideas of our age.

We could have had great leaders: there were men in our South with the intelligence, the integrity, the vision to become great leaders but we, the people, did not give them our support. We gave that support, every time, to the cheap, foul-mouthed demagogue who appealed not to our reason and conscience but to our anxiety; who begged us to return with him to the past, a past that never actually existed, instead of going on with the rest of mankind into the future. We let down our leaders by not building them up. A leader cannot be built up unless the people, the best people of a region, build him.

But it is not too late. We can still do it. The Negro group is searching for and finding its good leaders and is beginning to give these leaders their support. What men some of them are! If the white group could only find a young leader to match the brains and heart, the integrity and vision, the courage, the energy, and imagination of young Martin Luther King. For young Dr. King knows what every leader of stature must learn: that the way is as important as the goal we seek. And he has chosen the good way of non-violence, of intelligence, and compassion, and good will. A young white leader working shoulder to shoulder with Martin Luther King could do much to transform our South; to turn the mob spirit into the civilized Christian spirit that we should have down here.

Now: back to you and me. We must go on painting our pictures, yes; for only by searching for the meaning life has for each one of us can we, ourselves, become human beings fit for a great age. Each of us must keep on searching for our personal view of this, our only experience of life. But we must also combine our efforts to see to it that the great ideas of our age have a chance to be acted out, to become strong enough to win over the irrational evil enemies and errors of our age. Remember we won't do the naming but we will pick the winner. Let's get to work and do it. Shall we? Let's find the new faith, the new compassion, the new understanding, and yes, the new existential doubt, too, that will send us on and give us the strength and the courage to do what needs to be done. Let's commit ourselves, deeply and completely, not to neurotic security but to the survival of man on this earth.

A Trembling Earth*

. . . Being an informal and brief account of the southern literary landscape as seen by one of its writers

My earliest memory of the American South, which is my home, is of an earth that trembled: the ground beneath my feet never seemed quite firm.

The street of the small town on which I lived was quiet and serene. It sheltered its upper-class white children in spacious homes and enclosed them by its ceremonials in a womblike intellectual complacency. But not far away was the Big Swamp—the "trembling earth," the American Indians called it—and I was aware of the existence of this swamp from my earliest years. I knew in that limitless place—as without dimensions to a child's eyes as is a dream—there were strange things unfamiliar to Main Street: Its dark waters were full of secret, slow movements of creatures one never saw and its earth trembled if you stepped on it: that earth was green and beautiful and luxuriant with tangled growth; and all year long, delicate

---

* Speech written for Paris radio in the late fifties.

glowing flowers bloomed there; but snakes hid under those flowers and panthers and bears crept round the shrubs and vines and tall, massive trees, and though the ground was firm and strong enough to bear the weight of trees, it trembled when a small child stepped on it. I was told there was no solid foundation of rock under its surface but only mysterious waters which flowed ceaselessly from an unknown source to an unknown destination, and I believed it. And this belief and these images crept slowly to the center of my imagination and took root there.

As I grew older, as I saw more and learned more and asked more, I felt the moral earth trembling beneath my pressing questions. And again, I was aware of mysterious and unplumbed currents flowing below the thin human reason and again I saw the movement in those dark waters of forces, threatening and cruel and eternally fascinating. But I knew, also, that those waters nourished the flowers and the great trees above it, and I could not forget this.

Beyond my home on Main Street, on the distant rim of the town, were the shabby cabins of the black folk. As a child I often slipped away from the security of the big houses and my white playmates and went to this rim to visit and I found it a place full of laughter and pain. I felt the deep physical rhythms of its people, shared their anguish and shame and was awed by their lightning-sharp anger and their faith in God's concern for them. Out of those rickety shanties came some of the dream figures who have lived in my imagination ever since those early years.

Across the street was the church, the abode of God. For many, He never left that Church but He visited in our household often. Both my mother and father seemed on intimate terms with Him. To my father, God was a Close Friend and helpful Business Adviser; to my mother, He was Big Brother whose eyes helped her watch for moral deviations in her children and especially for those evils that concerned the body image. My own image of God was a confused blend of my parents' conceptions; and yet, beyond this naive montage there was another, ever-growing idea of God which I held to: something larger than the Big Swamp, even larger than cosmic space, and yet something closer which concerned me personally as a member of the human race. At the same time, I knew God was, for most of those who lived in my town, simply a White man of extraordinary size who was Overseer of all the dark forces in human nature which He kept under control by threats and magic barriers. And I knew the word, segregation, was to these neighbors and playmates and their parents not only a defense which they, themselves, had set up against the Negro race, but a holy ritual created by their white God to keep all things, dark and awesome, in their place. And I understood the South's anxiety, although I did not share it, when the barriers began to fall.

With these childhood memories and experiences and the insights of my maturity, it was natural, I think, for me to create in my books human beings who were torn and ambivalent, afraid of mysterious forces within their own depths yet secretly fascinated; obsessed by a cruelly Puritan conscience, yet compelled to act out their obscene fantasies; longing to love God even as they worshipped their own image: Men and women, struggling to come to terms with the Big Swamp of the mythic mind and with contemporary reality and with unnamed cosmic forces and possibilities; struggling with the good and the evil, the black and the white of their daily experiences.

These figures which I have created and set against the southern landscape are totally unlike William Faulkner's. His characters never struggle with themselves or with their world. They do not dream of God and they make no attempt, therefore, to hold a dialogue with Him. They are moral sleepwalkers. Faulkner seems to be able to bring his dream figures to life only after he has stripped them of brains and intelligence, drained off compassion and hope and longing, stamped out the poetry in them and excised their conscience. Once he has reduced them to moronic pygmies bereft of dreams he can do fabulous things with them. Whether it is worth the doing, I have never been quite sure.

Richard Wright, on the other hand, creates not dehumanized figures that never existed but men and women involved in a struggle larger than their own small lives. He limits this struggle almost entirely to that of the Negro's fight for freedom but in the telling of his stories the concept of human freedom grows complex and ambiguous. Most of his characters are Negroes; he has rarely created a white character of real interest. I feel that Wright sees depths and moral possibilities he has not, as yet, come to creative terms with. But one keeps watching him for he writes with power and honesty and profound insight.

In *All the King's Men*, the best of Robert Penn Warren's novels, we have been given a memorable portrait of a southern demagogue, and in the doing of it, Warren has painted in sharp, bold strokes our southern form of political totalitarianism.

In the generation younger than ours there are a group of writers who have turned away from the larger aspects of the human experience and have chosen small fragments to write about. Carson McCullers has done her most delicate and discerning work when writing of the loneliness of the child who is different. I say this, even as I concede freely that her most brilliant piece of writing, technically, is her *Ballad of the Sad Cafe*. Tennessee Williams, in sharp reaction to a South that demands strict conformity on every level of life, writes with a naked honesty of the sexually different and their agonizing struggles with a shadowy Norm which they seem never able to come to terms with. Capote chooses a variety of deviants and handles them with more wit and subtlety and less passion, and less moral concern, than does Williams. Ralph Ellison, close to the age of these others, has little in common with their point of view, save in his concern for the racially different. He has given us only one portrait—but a fine one—of an artist with a dark skin beating his imagination to pieces against a white unseeing, unhearing Wall.

Limits of time make it impossible for me to discuss Thomas Wolfe or Eudora Welty or our youngest group of writers. A few of the young ones stand out because of their fine writing talent but these talented few are presently writing of trivial matters. They are, as Malcolm Cowley says, "the indifferent ones." Afraid to let themselves become too concerned with the agony and the dreams and potentialities of modern man in a modern nightmare world. However, there are others: perhaps of less talent, certainly much less developed in their skills, who are intellectually aware of the human ordeal as we are now experiencing it, and passionately concerned. Whether they will leave an imprint on the South's literature, I don't know; they will surely affect the South's future, for they are reaching out philosophically, they are taking a moral stand and taking it with courage. And I think it is important to mention them, even so briefly as this.

OUT OF NEW CREATIVE TENSIONS

WILL COME PEACE[*]

It is as human to strive for peace as to pursue happiness but it is also human, I think, to fail in both endeavors unless we think more of consequences than goals.

For peace and happiness are presences, not objects we can grasp and hold to. They are our moments of grace which fall upon us at the height of creative tension when we make something good: a painting, a poem, a relationship; or when we discover a sliver of knowledge, or find meaning for our age in old symbols or new; or when we extend awareness of the depths and heights of human possibilities, or feel for an instant a sense of the numinous; or when we open a door where there was no door. At such times there comes to the maker, the discoverer, the doer a certainty that life is good. "It has meaning for me."

This is peace, as I think of it. Not cessation from struggle; not comfort, not absence of friction or controversy or ordeal—but freedom for men to maintain the maximum of creative tension, to go on

---

[*] Article in *Saturday Review*, December 24, 1960.

with the Quest, with the work, to engage in further dialogue with one's self and the others, to seek new forms in art and science, to look for, and now and then find, fresh simplicities in the old chaos.

But how is this kind of life possible in a world where the Terror grows ever larger! It isn't, of course. We must have disarmament, we must find ways to control nuclear weapons—and soon. For time is running out. (The horror is that such statements are already clichés that men, in apathy, turn away from.)

Are we sure we want a new life, a new vision—even though without it we cannot release the moral and intellectual energy needed to bring about conciliations on which world disarmament depends? Is it that we have actually, as some say, lost our commitment to the future? Or is it that we have not had, up to now, leaders who in tapping their own adrenals and imagination can tap ours, too?

Questions slide into a kind of death-clinch and we wonder what answer can break it. For each hard necessity is contingent upon an equally hard necessity and so it goes. No wonder we feel locked in a nightmare.

We can blame a thousand enemies for the condition we moderns are in. We can say it is caused by man's realization of the size of his universe, his recent grasp of the magnitude of time, his unadmitted knowledge that power to destroy us may fall at any time into the hands of an idiot. We can say it has to do with a shrunken vocabulary that fails to communicate with what is unproved in human existence; we can blame our loneliness on our loss of God; we can paint, draw, write of human fragmentation; we can root our troubles in the eighteenth century's overesteem of reason and the nineteenth century's overesteem of science and both centuries' underesteem of the non-rational and unknowable. Or we can blame it on the Communists if we are white and Western; or, if dark or Eastern, we can blame it on colonialism and American segregation. Or, if we are Communist, we can blame it on Capitalism's callous disregard of mass poverty. We can use the words of Buber or Sartre or Kierkegaard or Jaspers or Marcel or Nietzsche or Marx or Tillich or

Freud or Jung or Binswanger, or we can use our own homegrown words—and it will all make good sense.

Even so, we have not exhausted the interlocking reasons for man's loss of faith in his fellow man, in his God, in his own strength as individual to cope with mobs and machines and statistical magnitudes and human hungers and human differences, and an unknown future.

So the dialogue between man and his predicament continues. As it should. For only thus can we gain the insight needed for the heart's work, as Rilke long ago reminded us. And only when heart and mind are working well together can the imagination grasp the structure, the bony articulation, of the modern dilemma.

But a time finally comes—and I think it is here—when we must turn away from our introspection and boldly lift ourselves into a new age and a new way of being. And this near-impossible feat can be brought about only by fusing knowledge and technics with those magic, non-rational feelings we call love, compassion, concern, faith, hope. We'll do what must be done not by proving it first but by daring to believe what we cannot yet (or perhaps ever) prove. We'll find courage to look at the new vision not by being brave but by wanting so much an earth fit for humans that we willingly risk our lives, even our prestige and popularity for it.

Let me say it this way: War is the human race's Number Two enemy. Number One enemy is the creeping, persisting, ever-widening dehumanization of man. This is the disease of which nuclear war may be the terminal symptom. When dehumanization has gone far enough, men will not find it possible to believe there are non-violent ways of bringing about understanding and conciliation; they will not perceive the big value, they will lose their belief in word and symbol because they have torn out the inner meaning of words, they have corrupted the symbols we cherish.

This is scary stuff, at least to me. We can never face and master our ordeal by working on one level at a time. We can do it only by an in-depth simultaneity of effort: of individual, group, nation. On every known level of experience artist, scientist, preacher, politician, teacher, laborer and industrialist, young and old must pool their talents and skills, their imagination and knowledge, their symbols and their technologies, their metaphors and their dreams, their hope and their compassion. All this for what? To create a new kind of person, a new kind of life on this earth—and in the doing to bring about a set of conditions in which disarmament will become possible. We know the "problem" of war cannot be solved. But it will be transcended. Inevitably, we shall abandon it as skill and discipline but only when we find new ways, new rituals of conciliating men's needs and their hungers, new tensions which give dramatic value to life.

This is what I believe about "peace." It is difficult to separate the novelist from the person or the person from the citizen as I think of my writing and that of others. We must do one thing as citizen, another as writer; but—and this is important—both kinds of activities are fused in the person. What we believe, what we are, has a profound effect upon the quality of our writing. Much nonsense is printed, today, about the needs of artists to isolate themselves from this historical period we live in with its challenges to spirit and brain and body and its importunate knocking on the heart with its hungers and needs. One hears, "Of course you can be a great poet and still be a fascist; you can write a great novel and still cling to nihilism or to segregation." I don't believe a word of it.

Let's look at "segregation." It is a word I am deeply concerned with. But is my concern limited to civil rights? or to the trite phrase, "the Negro problem?" or to colonialism? or even to the "white problem?" No. Segregation, for me, is far more. It means the cleavage Western mind has dug between subject and object; it means loss of communication with our own self; it means that estrangement from God which oppresses modern man; it subsumes all the fragmentations of modern times. It is a symbol into which a thousand meanings may be read. For man is not solid animal but a creature whose symbols, while making him human have split him off from himself. In the act of symbolizing he steps far enough away to watch and wound himself; he walks into time and space and walks out, knowing his exit is called *death*. He is tortured by great separations but in his agony he creates relationships that bridge those separations; and then he builds his tower so he may look into the abyss he has just spanned and still dreads. Abyss and tower: both, Erich Kaller reminds us, are to be embraced in an encircling recognition. And this, too, has to do with peace.

When I think of the novel's contribution to peace, I think more of characters and metaphors than of subject matter; more of chasms and relationships than of war. There have been good novels that convince us of the futility of war. Too many to name. For me, this century's most powerful indictments of mass bombing are Hersey's documentary *Hiroshima* and Picasso's *Guernica*; *Hiroshima* leaves us shaken by human suffering and we move closer to its people; *Guernica* leaves us stone-cold with horror and we step back from dehumanized man as if from a cobra.

One of the greatest novels about "peace" is, for me, *Moby Dick*. Every tension in this book we feel, today; every dichotomy in its characters we understand. Melville's symbols of "whiteness" are fresh with spine-chilling meaning: his grasp of the mythic mind is superb and relevant to our understanding of today's mass man. Another book is Dostoievski's *Idiot*. Prince Myshkin might, right now, be taking part in the sit-ins in the South.

A novel's symbols and its myth are important, yes; but more than all else, its importance lies in how much of the future is in its characters, how many of its tensions will be shared and understood by readers who come after us. Regardless of its subject matter, a novel that meets these tests, will make its contribution to the new being, the new life our earth sorely needs.

THE MOB AND THE GHOST*

* * *

I don't remember when I first heard the word, segregation, but I knew its meaning from babyhood. I felt its pain when I was separated from people I loved for reasons I did not understand. Once it was death that caused the separation; once it was race. Both seemed equally mysterious to me.

But as I became a little older, I learned of another kind: I realized there were deep chasms between me and what I wanted to know: the *real things* I longed to understand. I began to suspect there were things I might never know. But I kept asking those old questions human beings have asked since they became aware they were human. And then, I discovered a devastating [fact]: the grown folks didn't know the answers, either. Even my mother and father were segregated from the Unknown—and this made me anxious. Why couldn't they explain birth to me? why couldn't they explain death: why couldn't they explain God? why didn't they know when eternity

---

* A talk given to the Students Colloquium of Emory University, April 27, 1961. ·

would end—which happened to be my obsessive question when I was nine years old. Why couldn't people tell you when you asked: Where did I come from? where am I going? who am I besides a name? why am I your child? what am I? why was I born? why must I die? why is God? and who? and where? what is all this living on the earth *for*? (We call them existential questions, today; but Socrates asked them long ago, and men in China and India and Judea and Egypt and Persia—and little children the world over.)

Separation from those we love—the cutting of the umbilical cord, the burial of the dead; and separation from the vast Unknown: these are the great, enduring prototypes of all other forms of human segregation. Perhaps, if we accepted them more completely, on deeper levels, we would not confuse superficial dichotomies, temporary fragmentations, or specific forms of segregation such as racial, with the unchangeable facts of the human condition.

We don't accept these prototypes because we do not ask the right questions about them. And sometimes we stop asking all the great questions simply because we cannot find their forms for our age— forms relevant to *us*, to you and me living in the middle of the twentieth century.

Do you remember Joseph K. in Kafka's *Trial*? who never asked the right questions about his arrest? Do you remember he never asked himself what *he* could do about it or what the arrest had to do with his own personal life; no—he could only ask others why *They* didn't do something about it? why wouldn't *They* get him out of this mess! He could only blame the Others for *their* corruption; he never looked inside at his own. Kafka was of my generation; he died young— wounded to death by despair as he watched his own countrymen ask the wrong questions again and again and again. He died before Hitler came to power but he knew Hitler was on the way, for a Hitler is always the answer to wrong questions when a whole people ask them. We in the South have so far settled for southern demagogues, and the Klan and the White Citizens Council, and apathy.

(I am tempted to digress here and comment on the wrong form of the questions now being asked by most of our writers and artists. I make an exception of Camus. They think they are asking the existential questions: but they, like Joseph K., are asking them in the wrong way. The philosophers have done better: long ago, Kierkegaard; and now Karl Jaspers, and Paul Tillich, and Marcel, and Martin Buber—and in a limited way, at certain moments, Sartre. But even the philosophers do not always find it easy to create the new forms of these questions that will speak to you and me.)

A question, no matter how important, is not right for us until we find its unique form for our place and time; we must find what links the question to our personal life. It is the specific we are after; the abstract must be changed into its many concrete shapes.

Let's find a specific form of the old question that is ours—ours because we have lived it and been hurt by it. It is this:

> Why at this critical turning point in history, as our planet is about to reach out to relate itself to other planets in outer space, are we now having so much difficulty relating to ourselves and each other? why have we turned our attention from soul to skin at this momentous time?

This question is no theory for you and me: its words wrap around our hearts and minds and tear our daily life to pieces. They could tear this university to pieces. Maybe the whole world. What are those words? Race . . . segregation . . . black . . . white . . . color . . . white supremacy.

All of us have been hurt by them; all have lost much of our freedom because of them.

Racial segregation first touched me when as a child I was not free to choose my little friends. It was then I learned a hard lesson: I learned to disesteem the colored people whom I deeply loved. I learned to give them the back-door treatment: to belittle them even as I cared for them; to clothe them in warm cheap sentimentality instead of the dignity and courtesy due them. Does it seem a trivial thing? Examine it closely: for love without esteem corrupts; backdoor treatment is humiliating to all who participate in it. Both leave stains on the soul.

Racial segregation touched me the second time when I felt it split my mind. It wasn't easy to believe in segregation and freedom simultaneously. It seemed crazy to me to talk of dignity and brotherhood and white supremacy in the same breath. But [it] scared me when I [saw] grown folks were affected, too. I slowly realized that they, too, did not dare ask the real questions or seek the real answers. I realized the words we were taught to love best, value most were actually hollow words—emptied of real meaning. Maybe somewhere they held meaning but not for us. At church, school, on the street, reading the newspapers, and watching politics I learned this. But what shook me was [that] my own parents [,who] taught me I was free and living in a great democracy, at the same time [taught me to be] a segregationist. How could I be free, if others were not free! What kind of sense did that make! But I dared not argue it. I knew my parents whom I believed in either didn't mean what they said or else were terribly mixed up. I decided they were just terribly mixed up, for I loved them; and I stopped thinking about it.

But it hurt inside. And my earth was once more trembling. And once more, I saw rivers that flowed so gently suddenly disappear; I saw ground that had been green and beautiful and on which I had played yesterday, suddenly sink and become a deep hole.

My third view of racial segregation came when I realized how it hurt and shamed Negroes. It is not easy for white people to realize a Negro has been hurt, not easy to feel the empathy of identification, but when I was ten years old, I at last felt it. I watched a little colored child whom I loved receive not only the back-door treatment but a much more cruel abandonment. And, once more, I was shaken hard. I knew the people I loved had done something wrong but because I loved them I couldn't admit it. So I lied like a crazy fool, defending them, identifying with them in blind, desperate loyalty; telling myself if they were cruel, it was all right to be cruel; if they said crazy, contradictory things, it was all right to do it. But it didn't work. I knew better.

I got my fourth view of this troubling question when I was twenty-four years old. I left the South and went to China. I lived three years in Chekiang province and there I saw the same old segregation I thought I had left behind. I collided in China with white colonialism. I heard the same old story but now it had a new accent, a sharper rhythm, different imagery. Somehow, it seemed more cruel because it was, [to me,] a new cruelty. Old cruelties never bother us much. It was, perhaps, a critical moment in my life: when my interior world finally began to reach out and tie itself to my exterior world. However that may be, the first time I saw a Chinese coolie brutally lashed on Nanking Road—in broad daylight—by a British policeman, my mind tore wide open. It has never closed up since.

Was it not to be expected that when I began to write in my early thirties I would write of life as I had experienced it? Not as a young woman born and reared in Paris might know life but as I, born and reared in the fragmented South, know it. I have been to Paris, yes; and to many places across the earth. But what I really know is what I have perceived from childhood with my senses and heart and felt in my muscles; what I have grasped intuitively and made into new living forms within my imagination.

I have never written about the Negro problem because I don't think there is one. There may soon be an African problem of inverse racism, patterned on the white man's, but let's pray it won't happen. No. * * * I have written of people split off from their future and sometimes from their own childhood. I have written of broken relationships, of torn integrities, of invisible walls against which we destroy ourselves.

To its author, *Strange Fruit* is first a novel, then second, a kind of parable of the children of light and darkness—and I do not mean skin color. We, the South's children, are the fruit [of the] tree White Supremacy has produced. Do you not see that we are something a bit strange? a wild bitter fruit that puckers the age we live in?

My second book, *Killers of the Dream*, was a personal kind of book about experiences which most southerners share with me. In it, I grappled with the hard questions. And as I searched past and present and stared hard at the future I found new meanings in our biracial culture. I began to see racism and its rituals of segregation as a symptom of a grave illness that is not limited to southerners but is suffered by the whole world. A world that seems to have lost its sense of human relatedness, its desire for communion.

When people think more of their skin color than of their souls, something has happened to them. What? and why? Are we sick because we have lost our sense of direction? because we have lost our human purpose? What has racial segregation to do with estrangement from God and what has estrangement from God to do with racial segregation? How does racism connect up with overesteem of technology and our pathetic craving for proof? what does it have to do with automation? anonymity? and the persisting dehumanization of our life? Is it not relevant to our sickness that hope and faith have become the dirty words of the decade? What has revived neonihilism in the spurious form the critics now dabble in? why is it so fashionable in literary circles to revere Ezra Pound? These are all symptoms, are they not? Racism happens to be only the most dangerous of them.

But let's come closer home. People cling to their color because they have nothing else to cling to. Look hard at rural and city slums. These people are obviously deprived and have been for a long time; deprived of housing, jobs, food, medical care. But deprivation is not limited to the poor. The rich—and we in the middle brackets—are also deprived people. Some of us are not hungry nor did we in childhood have rickets and pellagra; but we suffered then and are suffering now from spiritual deprivation. The disease that has attacked so many of us is partly due to the fact that man is no longer proud of being man. I do not think anyone, anywhere, rich or poor, educated or ignorant, clings to racism if he is sure of himself as a person. It isn't fear of intermarriage, it is fear of the emptiness inside us that makes some of us cling to segregation. We lean against the wall to keep from falling flat on our faces.

Once you touch your own humanity, once you value your personal differences, once you begin to exist, to relate yourself to your world, to think, to accept what you find inside you; once you begin to feel compassion and concern for others, you are no longer merely a white man or white woman: you are a person, and being a person, you don't need segregation.

A racist is in trouble; he is sick; education won't help him any more than it will help a man sick with cancer. Somebody should have the education—the civic leaders and parents of small children, and the governor maybe, and university boards, but it is too late for the racist to benefit from it.

And now, we begin to see that racism is not only symptom, it is a symbolic substitute for something men desperately need and do not have. Our skin color is *something that stands for something else.* And the *something else* is what concerns us. We begin to see that the ritual of segregation is a cluster of symbolic acts. We begin to catch on that *darkness* and *whiteness* are symbols living on many levels of our life.

And now, let us look at the symbol and the mob together; for they are close kin, and often seen in each other's company.

The mob at Athens, last January, was behaving not logically, not rationally, but symbolically. Did those students who threw stones at Charlayne Hunter hate the girl as a real individual? did they know her? had they ever talked with her? No. But she had come into their lives and her presence had become a profound threat to them. Now how was she threatening them? I can understand it only in this way: Charlayne Hunter, whom they did not know, was threatening them because she had become a ghost. She had lost her identity as a girl and had turned like magic into a giant-size ghost. The name, "Charlayne Hunter," did not disturb them—it was other names, other words that lay half-sleeping in their minds. This young freshman had without knowing it become Someone who stands for Something Else. Suddenly, she was a *symbol* of images, impulses, feelings, memories they dreaded; she was the ghost who embodied these dreads. She was the Return of the Repressed.

People have asked all over the world why it took 2,000 students to stone a girl when one could have done it alone? But that is the wrong question, for the students were not stoning a *girl*, they were stoning memories, fantasies. One student could easily have killed her. But nobody wanted to kill this girl, they wanted to kill a ghost. And ghosts are not easy to kill; also they scare us. No wonder two thousand students ganged up together to do it. Ghost hunting—and witch hunting—is always done by mobs.

What is a mob, actually? We say the word, and tend to think of a crowd of people. But a mob is not a crowd: it is a state of mind.

I was caught once in a crowd of two million people in Delhi; pushed along for a mile as if by a great wind. But those two million Indians did not make a mob. On the contrary, they were a happy crowd celebrating Republic Day. Excited? yes; but excited not by hate and dread but by pride and happiness. They were related to each other by love for their country and belief in it. Related. Not fused into something solid.

And they were relaxed because a good future was opening up. Relaxed enough to listen to their children's talk, to compliment each other, to laugh at funny things. They were observant, reacting with curiosity, pride, appreciation. You can't make a mob out of people who are interested in a variety of things and feeling a variety of emotions. A mob is interested in only One Thing, it feels only One Feeling. It is solidified, it is monolithic.

Now—suppose those two million people pushed tight against each other had suddenly grown frightened. There would have been panic and many would have been trampled to death. But even then, we couldn't have called that crowd a mob. For a stampeding, panicky crowd hurts each other unintentionally while a mob has an object it *wants to hurt*.

The size of the crowd has little to do with a mob. Two or three people, even one can become a mob. For a mob begins in a man's mind. Mood is therefore important. How people feel about the future is important. But the thing to remember is this: to make a mob in the street you must collect people who think one thing and feel one emotion; they must also be idol worshipers. No one who worships God can qualify as a member of a mob. Mob members are religious but they worship idols. To sum it up: they worship an idol, they think one thing, feel one way, fear the future, and want to hurt somebody.

The basic difference in a mob and a crowd lies, therefore, in the quality of [its] people.

A mob always begins inside us: never is it an outside job. Always it is an inside job: the troublemakers are there, but they are inside you and me.

A mob depends, therefore, on the state of mind of every individual near enough to become a part of the mob. If everybody has a different state of mind, different interests and beliefs, you can't solidify these differences into a mob. Your best protection against mobs here at Emory is for everybody to think for himself and be different, to vary in beliefs, and to avoid the worshiping of idols. But, remember, I am speaking of real states of mind, not pretended ones. The point is: you've got to solidify a mob, you've got to make it monolithic, and you can't do it if there are all sorts of ideas on the campus and a wide variety of attitudes, and feelings. Now, if you want to be an efficient mob member, here is the recipe: First, you strip off your reason and whatever you've learned about the world and yourself—it probably isn't much; then you strip off your conscience and your human values; then your sense of responsibility; then you peel off your good taste, your belief in fairness, your sense of humor and all such feelings as compassion, kindness, etc. Then you strip off every bit of your courage and hide your name. When you do all this you are ready to be a mob member; maybe, you can be leader of the mob. For you are now pretty close to your mythic mind, the ancient nub of *homo sapiens*—the part of you that began developing more than a million years ago and the part of you out of which mobs come. * * *

But however complete the stripping act may be, you haven't become an animal. It is a mistaken idea to speak of a mob as a great prehistoric animal even though it does behave like one. For the fact is: no matter how hard man tries he can't become an animal. He becomes something more horrible—a dehumanized man. Animals are vastly superior to a dehumanized man. For man, in order to dehumanize himself, has to try to reverse what is irreversible. In the attempt, we pervert, cripple, poison ourselves and others; we hurt, we injure. We become horrifying but we don't ever become mythic man again.

When man tries to split himself into fragments, when he tries to strip off all he has learned and become, when he tries to get rid of his love and compassion and conscience, catastrophe is ahead. His destination is likely to be either death for others or insanity for himself. Look at Eichmann. Look at the other Nazis. They tried to separate the rational mind from a sense of right and wrong, and from love and compassion. They tried to keep reason and scientific method together but separated from concern for humanity. We know what happened to Jews and Nazis and the Germans who collaborated actively or sometimes, as we do in the South, by closing eyes and ears. We know and are aghast at its horror.

You see, the Nazis couldn't do what they intended to do. For what happened? When the moral controls were taken down, when human values were thrown away, when love was discarded, scientific method began working hand in hand with hate and the mythic mind.

Reason can't work alone. It is in itself only a technic, a bundle of skills, a way of thinking—the scientific method is only a highly disciplined activity of the reason. But it doesn't work by itself: it needs energy, and if one kind of energy is cut off, it finds another.

The truth is, reason can't move very far without feelings—for out of emotion comes energy and it shouldn't go far without human values, for its purpose is determined by those values. Conscience is not expendable in human affairs at any time. But reason and its technic, the scientific method, also cannot function without drawing from the mythic mind. For out of the mythic mind comes our power to symbolize, and our power to dream, and our power to invent. It, too, is not expendable in human affairs.

This is the point: none of the functions of the human personality can be safely split off or abandoned: they must work together. Whatever morality we have is based on this one truth: we can't segregate parts of our nature or learnings from each other. The essence of morality, the essence of human health, lies in our keeping in a related whole (a) the mythic mind; (b) the reason; (c) the emotions; (d) the conscience, when it is oriented not to authority but to human values. We shall lose our health, our creative powers, our capacity to grow, our grasp on the human future if we segregate those parts of the Self from each other.

But the Nazis tried to do it. They tried to reverse the irreversible. They tried to turn back human evolution. It couldn't be done. But they killed six million Jews, and did it ruthlessly and coldly and methodically, and scientifically. And easily—for when they separated themselves from their human conscience and obeyed German authority instead of the soft voice of God (which never screams but only whispers), when they separated themselves from love, then hate and the mythic mind linked up to the scientific method—and produced what we are now seeing in its details for the first time: a monstrous, massive killing of the human spirit. Can Germany ever recover? I am not sure.

We commit a profound sin, maybe an unpardonable one, when we attempt to reverse the irreversible in man's nature. Man has slowly evolved into a human being; it has taken him a million years to get to where he is now; and only for ten thousand years (or less) has he participated in his own evolution. Just a little participation at first; then more, and still more as he created the human language, and ways of recording it, and created art, and tools; then Western man pushed forward like a rocket when he dared try to discover his earth and the cosmos, to go on the quest for knowledge; when he discovered time and the historical method. And then came Western music; and then came more and more technology and more and more discoveries which we call modern; and along with all this, Western man was dreaming of the importance of the person; he began to consider freedom necessary to this person; and he began to believe this person had rights.

Now man is on his own: God has apparently freed him: freed him to destroy himself and the human race if he wants to or to make it something unimaginably great and wonderful; freed him to tear human nature or to fuse it into a beautifully organized working whole; freed him to lose his health and sanity or to strengthen his soul and body—freed him to make the human race a superb Creation or a monstrosity. But man is not free to break God's laws—he cannot—and hence he is not free to move backward in evolution: to reverse the irreversible.

But a mob tries to do this; and the Nazis tried; and the Klan tries; and the White Citizens Councils try; and the Birchites are trying. They all try to make the mythic mind supreme in man's nature.

It is fascinating to study the mythic mind. I think few have done a better job of analyzing it than did Ernst Cassirer, the great German philosopher who died a few years ago in this country—a refugee from Hitler.

Let's give it a closer look: You are familiar with how the reason works: you know it deals with time and space, and cause and effect; you know it values facts, you realize it is basically a skill we begin developing in babyhood; you realize it has its disciplines and its technics, and scientific method is only one of these. We learn to reason, for we are not born knowing how. But we are born with our mythic mind working. And it doesn't change its way of working, having learned it nearly a million years ago. It never heard of logic; it disregards time and space; in the mythic mind you can be in two or three places at the same time or you can be in two different hours separated from each other by twenty years. And it is quite possible that you may even be somewhere ten thousand years distant at the same time you are in this minute. It is possible. The mythic mind also likes to confuse coincidence with cause and effect. It likes to have a lot of things happening simultaneously. You know something about simultaneity in modern art—this, of course, came straight out of the mythic mind.

But the quality that fascinates me most about the mythic mind (because I catch it happening to me quite often) is its *melting* quality: it can spread like warm molasses all over the universe. For instance:

the mythic mind loves to extrapolate one aspect of a person, a situation, an event, and merge it with that same aspect wherever it finds it. It likes to *spread*, to merge. (It is obvious that "guilt by association" comes out of the mythic mind.)

But let's watch it work on the quality we call "whiteness." The mythic mind picks it up and begins spreading it in all directions, reaching out and naming all people who happen to have a white skin as the same kind of people. Now your reason tells you at once that this isn't so. Most of us in this room are white. But are we the same? We differ in intelligence; we differ in our glandular organization (which is far more important to our chance of achievement than is our color). We differ in blood pressure, blood count, enzymes, blood type, the number of antibodies in our blood, our tendency to take diseases, the rate of heartbeat, our muscular reflexes; we differ greatly in our memories and in the values our consciences cherish; and in our courage to meet ordeals, and in our sense of humor, and our talents. In what, then, does the sameness of white people consist? Only one thing: their skin color. For actually, we may or may not be a living part of this great Western culture we've looked at so briefly. Some of us are no more than dead stuff carried along by Western culture. Whether we do or don't contribute to it has nothing to do with our skin color. The only other common character we white-skinned people possess is a small something in our genes which will likely let our children inherit a more or less white skin. That is all.

Our reason tells us this, having already collected this knowledge for us. Reason knows that whiteness does not make us the same, and that to say so is nonsense. But the mythic mind adores nonsense just as do children. It is bored by facts, so it goes ahead shouting that all people with white skins are The Same. And then it dares brag that the sameness is good, even holy.

But is it? The rational layer of the mind, supported by science, tells us it is our differences that are important to human evolution. Nature has never carried all her eggs in one basket. She—as does science—values real differences, not superficial ones. The shape of

the hands has been far more important to our achievements and survival on this earth than any group's skin color.

But though the mythic mind can't reason or think straight, it loves
to symbolize—just as do painters, good story tellers, musicians. As
do you and I. Not only do art and stories come out of the mythic
mind, all human symbols, all dreams, all hypotheses begin there—
as does poetry, as does religion. We, as a human race, would die
without our symbols; indeed, we should never have become human.
And it is also—call it unconscious or mythic mind—a rich reservoir
full of old dreams and new ones, and all kinds of things out of the
great million-year-old Human Experience; full of biological and
spiritual wisdom.

But it is full of dangers, too. Tremendous dangers. One is: its
amazing energy which drives body and mind and comes out of its
easy union with emotions. It is full of strength—the stuff survival
and life itself is made of.

It is powerful in the same way atomic energy is powerful—and as
dangerous when we are not protected from it. We need seven feet of
concrete and plenty of lead between us and it. And it is also loaded
with good potentialities. Like atomic energy it can create and destroy. To live with either we must protect ourselves.

We achieve protection from mythic activities by setting up a complex system of controls which emanates from reason, compassionate
love, conscience, knowledge—all, working together, all reinforcing
each other and motivating each other, and protecting each other.

As long as the mythic mind stays within the places it belongs—art,
books, inventions, religion, scientific theory, poetry—it is all right.
But when it begins to step out as symbolic acting we'd better watch
out. For then it is that the controls begin slipping. Whenever the
mythic mind *acts*, some of the controls loosen a little. It may be a
fine thing; but we need to watch it. Symbolic acting is necessary to
man; the danger is that it may be misinterpreted or misunderstood if
it steps outside its frame. The safest frames for symbolic acts are: the
stage, picture frame, museum, book cases, and church and labora-

tory. For the reason assumes that action belongs in its domain and it tries to interpret all acts, even symbolic acts, as rational ones. But we know symbolic action is nothing of the sort.

All of you have known a child who, insecure, unhappy, steals symbolically. You understand, do you not, that she is actually stealing something; it isn't happening in her imagination. But though she may steal money or a watch or a pin, she is symbolically stealing something else. What she wants and needs is love, and security. What she does—and it is a highly creative act—is to transform in her mythic mind that money or watch or pin into parental love and security. You remember Rumpelstiltskin? the dwarf who transformed straw into gold? Well, the mythic mind loves its fairy stories; and the little girl is acting one out.

In a sense, that is exactly what a mob does: it acts out a fairy story, a grim one usually—but then fairy stories are often grim.

And now, let's turn away from art and race and from segregation on all its levels, and from little girls who steal, and look briefly at a love affair. Yours, maybe. If you fall in love only in your mythic mind, if your girl becomes for you only a symbol for something else, then God help you. If you love only with your conscience and your reason, if you let *them* pick out your girl, then God help *her.* It takes all of you to have a real love affair. It takes all of me to write a good book or to create anything real and new. But the kind of person who keeps the whole of himself together—drawing on all of it—is not going to be found anytime, anywhere in a mob.

WORDS THAT CHAIN US
AND WORDS THAT SET US FREE*

We who are writers spend our days battling words and cajoling them, scolding and pleading. We cannot do without them and yet we cannot depend on them. They bewitch us and betray us, they give us courage, and they imprison us, they comfort, and then they scare us half to death; and sometimes, they destroy us by persuading us they are mirrors when actually they are painted walls.

There are, of course, fine things to be said for words when used by those who know how. A poet can perform miracles by using words as symbols—because he knows he is using them that way. But a word used symbolically by the man in the street who thinks he is using it factually or literally can get the whole world in trouble. With words you should know what you are doing.

For instance, the word "white." A member of the Citizens Council does not mean by that word what a painter means. The painter is using the word literally. When he says "white" he means white. But when a Citizens Councilman or Klansman or Birchite says "white"

* Article in *New South*, March 1962.

he is using it symbolically and he may mean anything; to know what he means you would need to understand his whole life, all he fears and dreads, all he wants to be like, all he doesn't want to be like, and heaven knows what else.

As I look back across the thirty-five years since I first became publicly involved in this awesome love-hate affair between the two races, which has invaded or been invaded by politics, economics, world survival, sex, family life, religion, art, mental health, literature, and narcissistic regard for our own image, it seems to me that much of our trouble can be blamed on the words we use. Especially have we been mired up in the careless use of symbols.

But it is more than mixing symbols and facts and things until we don't know which is which; we also have a curious tendency to use words inappropriately. The word "equality" is a case in point. But let's leave it, just now.

Let's look at a phrase that was being tossed around quite a bit when I first got involved: the *Negro problem*. People loved to talk about the *Negro problem*—at least those who would talk at all. Even Negroes talked about the *Negro problem*. Trotting a few paces behind this phrase was another (new for those days): the *minority problem*. Had you not known better, you would have thought that Negroes, as Negroes, were real problems to the rest of the world; and you would have thought (and many did) that any minority group no matter what composed of—artists, geniuses, Jews, scientists, or whooping cranes—was ipso facto, a "problem." About this time, too, there was a good bit of talk about *intercultural relationships*, as though one human being could have intercultural relations with another. (Not much of this got into the South; and I praise southerners for at least having enough sense to know that however messy our relationships were with each other, at least we wouldn't try "intercultural" ones.)

But it was really the problem of "the Negro" and "the minorities" that threw me. The indoctrination given all southern children from birth by means of jokes, actions, statements, rituals, whispers, et cetera, must not have taken well with me. For I could not understand why Negroes (or minorities) were a problem. To whom: To ourselves? Well, maybe; we are all problems to ourselves. But why to us? Wasn't it really that *we* were problems to *them?*

But you must admit it was clever of whoever thought it all up. For that phrase, the *Negro problem*, by being used seriously dumped the whole moral and cultural burden on the Negro population while white folks slid out from under their obligations.

But a time came when the phrase began to drop out of people's talk. And it happened because a few honest men and women began to get a new view of the situation. What they saw was so plain it now embarrasses one to remember that for so long it was not plain. What did they do? They realized that the killer is the problem, not the man killed; the oppressor is the one for folks to put the handcuffs on, not the oppressed; the thief who steals a man's rights is the one to do time in jail, not the man whose rights have been stolen. That phrase, the *white problem*, had crept into our minds cautiously, but once there, it stayed.

This was a real breakthrough, or the beginning of a breakthrough. The use of the phrase has been a painful thing to white people, North and South, and its implications are still not very clearly understood (as a study of jail-ins and newspaper editorials will suggest); but it has sunk deep enough into literate minds that few, today, would be caught talking about this "Negro problem."

The idea moved slowly but it moved. This began in the late 1930s and early 1940s. A subtle transformation gradually took place. More and more people began to speak of "our moral responsibility." More and more glances were turned on the white group by its own members, and the question: *Why has this happened?* was asked, again and again.

Now, not many wanted to know the real answer. But they did want some kind of answer to stop the questions which had begun to sneak down close to the heart. So, they made a quarter-turn back and looked at "the Negro" again.

During the thirties, you remember, we had quite a flurry of fall-out from Marxist activities in this country; all sorts of theories and words were floating around; it was easy to pull a handful out of the atmo-

sphere and declare, "The Negro problem is a matter of economics."
It is amazing how this seemed to ease the nerves not only of whites
but of blacks, too. By depersonalizing "the Negro" and turning him
into an "economic problem," by making him a sort of monkey
wrench in the Capitalist machine, it gave some Negroes emotional
distance from their trouble (rather hard to see why, but it did) and it
made white folks forget that Negroes would bleed if you cut them and
Negro children would grow wizened and bitter without bread and
dignity.

That word *dignity* might have shaken everybody awake, except
that it was just then not being used. Its use came a bit later, along
with talk of "human rights" and "human relationships." Without
realizing we were moving, we had turned and were looking in another direction. There, before us, the human being loomed like a
giant. *Human rights . . . human dignity.* White Supremacists were
stunned by the words; they were too big to climb over and too solid to
slip through. To any sensitive person who looked and listened the
notions about "superiority" and "inferiority" began to seem shabby
and sleazy.

(Let me say this: semantics is not a magic wand, for me. Whether
fresh insight comes first or fresh words I don't know. To this day, I
am as bemused by the hen and the egg dilemma as I was at six years
old. But I know this: when we begin to get new insight we tend to
find new words, for only by using the new can we, in turn, communicate the new insight to others or even to ourselves. Surely there
is a simultaneity about this matter of fresh phrases gushing out of our
vocabulary and fresh ideas gushing into our minds. A new *gestalt* is
formed, a new coming-together of multiple forces [internal and ex-
ternal] takes place and this *gestalt* transforms us and the situation in
which we exist.)

It is strange and wonderful to think something you have never
thought before, and to find the right words in which to say it. Your
mind knows when the steel corsets we call stereotypes have come off.
I remember the excitement that swept over me when in thinking
about our South and our twisted ambivalent relationships, I sud-

denly saw what was new to me. It was this: I realized that race relationships, like sex relationships, take on the quality of our other relationships. If our sex relationships are troublesome and ambiguous,
we can be pretty sure some of our non-sexual relationships are even
more troublesome and ambiguous. If we bow easily to authority in
the matter of racial segregation which, in our hearts, we believe is
morally wrong, we shall in other matters, too, bow to authority even
when our conscience does not agree. If we feel all right about giving
Negroes the back-door treatment, we probably feel all right about
giving it to quite a few other people. If a superficial difference like
skin color disturbs us to the extent that we are willing to injure or let
be injured those different in color from us, then we are probably
willing to injure those who hold different opinions or values.

I began to see that a man's quality affects all his relationships and
all his relationships affect his quality.

This hurting insight (and it did hurt), this illumination of an obs-
cure corner in human affairs, came to me, one summer, while I was
directing a camp for children. In that camp we talked often about
"life." While these children and I searched together for wisdom (they
did it with such candor and dignity) I began to see, as I wrote in *Killers of the Dream*, that racial segregation is both a symbol and a
symptom of a way of life that affects us on all levels of our being. I
began to see how the numberless strands are interwoven: you bring
about racial segregation only by bringing about intellectual segregation; if you split a child off from other people by insisting that it
follow the rituals of racial arrogance, then you should know you are
splitting the child off from knowledge of itself, from values which
democratic, ethical men cherish, and from thousands of creative
relationships with its world.

If you segregate—I continued this dialogue with myself for
months afterward—then you should realize that people on both sides
of the sign, the curtain, the chasm are equally hurt by the act. Suddenly, my mind felt warm and full of electricity as happens when I
am giving up old ideas and thinking new ones.

I saw, not only with mind but with heart and imagination, that every white child is as injured by the ritual and ideology of segregation as is the Negro child.

I remember well when I first said it aloud, in a public place. (I had written it—indeed, *Strange Fruit,* and many columns in *South Today* in 1938, '39, and on are full of its implications—but I had not said it in public places.) I was trembling as I stood in that "white" church in Raleigh, North Carolina in 1943.* I told that audience about our children at camp and some of the questions they found no right answers for. Then I spoke of segregation: of the frame on which we have pinned our children, white and Negro: each on its own side of the frame, each distorted in its own way, but all crippled by what we call our southern way of life. It was such a simple thing to say, was it not? such an obvious truth? But you see, the ritual of segregation cuts us off from simple obvious truths and along with the ritual goes, like a policeman, the taboo against questioning.

After this speaking aloud, I felt free. I could turn in all directions and look at what I saw. I found myself becoming irritated and bored by the "proofs" sociologists and anthropologists and psychologists were producing which told us "the Negro race is equal to the white race." My reaction was: What does it matter! What matters is the harm segregation is inflicting on every child regardless of its race; what matters is the damage we are doing to our own minds, souls, consciences, hearts, as well as to others.

So—I threw *equal* out of my vocabulary. I don't think it matters two cents who is equal to whom. No individual is equal to another individual. We cannot be. It is not in our nature to be the same. All growing things are different—but men are obviously different; and become men because of their differences.

Equal and *equality* as they relate to the individual were now useless to me. But I held on to *equality* and *equal* as they relate to men's rights as citizens, as human beings. I learned to say it this way: Men have the right to be different but they also have the right to an equal opportunity to live fully and freely, for *as human beings* they

---

* See above, "Children and Color," p. 30.

belong to the human race, and are of the same importance before God. After we had begun to talk rather often and freely about human dignity, human freedom, human rights, it seemed emotionally logical to speak of *the human family*. In a good family, as everyone on earth knows, difference and sameness are not concepts that hold much relevance. In a family, one gives each member what that member's development seems to need and one asks of that member what he is able to give.

The semantic journey from "the Negro problem" to "the human family" suggests how our collective thinking and feelings have developed during a period of three decades or more.

But, even though many now find it natural to think in these more human terms there are others who somehow seem frozen to concepts of "superiority" and "inferiority"—as though such were measurable.

Perhaps one of the silliest and most dangerous of tests is the so-called intelligence test. When this testing got going, back in the 1920s, it did not require experts to see holes and slits in this paper wall that purported to separate intelligent people from those not so intelligent. This, in itself, is a form of segregation that might wisely be scrutinized. But regardless of the ethics of the situation, there were so many obvious fallacies in the methodology and the concept. The men who devised the tests based them on what they and others like them knew about life; not even on what I knew about life, or you; and certainly not on what Einstein or Socrates or Dante or Lao Tse, or Leonardo or Cleopatra, or Kierkegaard knew about the human experience; or what the Hindus knew or the wise old chiefs of African tribes knew. Culture is too complex, knowledge is too undulating, both are too interlocking and yet volatile and ambiguous to be pulled out to a straight measuring line.

What really happened was that the machine age seduced these testers. Living in a time when machines were everywhere, it somehow became easy for the testers to think of men as though they were refrigerators or cars: something made, not something living and changing from day to day. It seemed reasonable to them to extrapolate the "intelligence" from the rest of the organism—at least, to try to. Since it was valid to test two washing machines and say one is more capable of doing a job than the other, it seemed valid, to them, to compare children or men. But the testers were not limiting their tests to job-efficiency, they thought they were testing the whole of men's intelligence.

They not only overlooked the ever-changing cultural differences, they forgot it isn't built of "parts." They even forgot plain old human nature. Only in recent years have testers caught on to the fact that many people don't like to be tested and refuse to give out what is asked of them. They overlooked the ones who just plain resent filling in blanks and who rage at having to choose one of four choices when they think maybe all four are wrong; and the even more stubborn ones among us who refuse to say "Yes" or "No" when neither is a fit answer to a question.

Now, today, due to the manic energy of the Birchites and certain Mississippians and certain neo-Nazis and a passel of White Supremacists, North and South, this matter of the "equality of the races" is being worked over again. The White Supremacists claim the testers did not really prove the "equality of the races." Of course they didn't—and few anthropologists, today, think such proofs are or probably can ever be valid. What the testers did find, when investigating the intelligence of "races," was that all races, as races, can learn well enough whatever the twentieth century can teach them about science, machines, politics, medicine, and the modern ways of making money and making war. What everybody is sure of, whether tester or non-tester, is that no race exists today that is not capable of making nuclear bombs—if not today, then tomorrow. This fact about "equal intelligence" is the only one we need be worrying about.

But the real answer to this talk of valid and invalid tests is that it simply does not matter. If you are morally civilized you treat people right regardless of their intelligence or their looks or their weakness or strength. You don't keep a crippled man from voting or riding the bus; you don't bar a poet from a restaurant because he is a genius and the rest of us are not; you don't cheat a child who can't count his money. You don't tell a rural man he can't come into a city store and be waited on, or that he cannot vote because he is not as sophisticated in the arts or literature as is an urban man. (Of course he may be more so.) But rural men in Georgia do actually keep urban men's votes from counting simply because they don't live in rural areas. And southern cities do keep Negro people out of hotels and theaters.

Thinking of these matters and the confusion so many feel, I have become convinced that *our right to be different* is, in a deep sense, the most precious right we human beings have, and the one most likely, if we hold to it, to ensure the human race a future. We need to treasure human differences where they are important (I can't see that skin color is more important than eye color); we need to cherish the unique achievements of various groups, to protect the unique talents of individuals, to value the various beliefs and ideas and abilities that seem to grow more easily in one culture than in another. We may need them all for our survival—certainly, we shall need some of them one of these days, and we don't know which we shall need the most or where they may come to birth.

It may be well, therefore, to remind ourselves that equal rights should not and need not lead to conformity; and to keep this clear, it is a good idea to hold in sight our civil liberties—for sometimes equal rights and civil liberties lock horns in small minds. In Russia, for instance, men's civil rights have been gained only by the loss of their civil liberties. While in Mississippi many white men think they can hold on to their civil liberties (they usually mean their personal liberty to do as they please) only by taking away from Negroes their civil rights.

This is a false dilemma. Actually, in a democracy, a man cannot hold on to his civil rights without the help of his civil liberties nor can he hold on to his civil liberties without his civil rights.

Every right carries with it specific obligations and responsibilities. Otherwise, the word "right" becomes a grim joke, a devilish trick played on the human mind.

As we grow in wisdom, we shall learn more but we, at least, know this much now: we know, however different, however good or evil, dull or bright, pleasing or obnoxious we may be as individuals, as human beings we share in a mystical sanctity. We are the handiwork of God, or if the word bothers you, of Something Big, bigger than we are, bigger than any race, any age, bigger than the Earth we live on. We are, somehow, related to ourselves, to each other and to this Great Source of All Life. We don't know the purpose of human existence but even though unknown, this purpose and this relationship lay an obligation on us to seek truth and excellence, to value knowledge and insight, to grasp *arete* and hold to it. Quality is as important to the human race as is equality; we cannot afford in our struggles for human rights to forget this human obligation laid on us at birth: to grow in wisdom and honor and compassion.

As these matters became more intimately real to me, in my search as a southerner for a good way of life, I found myself thinking of segregation in a more philosophical sense. Segregation was to me no longer simply a "problem" if you want to use that word; not simply a wall, a chasm, a ritual, but it is the essence of the human condition. For we are all segregated from ultimate knowledge; and birth and death are two archetypal forms of segregation, which we shall experience but never know we experience. These are Great Separations that we cannot change. And it is out of them, out of the meaning of birth and death, out of our hunger to know and to understand that all the great questions have come: *Who am I? Why was I born? Why am I your child? What is eternity? Who is God? Why is death?* These are ancient and unanswerable questions about human existence, about its meaning, its purpose. But in our attempts to answer them we have learned to ask the smaller questions of science which can be answered, we have learned to make discoveries and explorations; and, too, out of these questions and the deep loneliness they engender have come art and poetry and music. The chasms are still there but we have bridged them. We have not found God but we have found in ourselves the power to keep reaching out for Him by relating to our own Self, and to others and to knowledge, and we have learned to keep our hearts on "ultimate concerns." We have become men, not because we have found [the] answers but because we still ask the questions, and in asking have learned, as I said in *The Journey*, "to live quietly with uncertainties."

We? all of us? No; and perhaps not one of us for more than a part of the time. But the searchers have at least learned that the unpardonable sin for the human race is to settle for small answers to the great questions. Here, right here, I think, lies the basic moral fact with which racists and segregationists and all ideologists must come to terms. We cannot ask *Who am I?* and answer that we are "white men." This is blasphemy as I understand its meaning. (Nor of course can we say that we are Negroes or Jews or Christians or Moslems or Hindus or Capitalists or Communists.)

I say this "from the mountain top" where all of us must spend some of our time in order to get a glimpse of a world view.

But when we go down to the streets and the market place and the legislative halls and the factories and the farms and the schools and the slums and hospitals, we run head-on into other reasons, cogent, concrete, painful, why our way of life is physically unhealthful and culturally debilitating and esthetically ugly and emotionally injurious. The naked fact, the inescapable situation, is that millions of men and women and children are shamed and hurt and smothered and chained by our segregated way of life. To a man, watching his child become stunted and psychically deformed because of lack of food and medicine and lack of esteem and lack of a place to play, the "great questions" will seem far away and not important. He will find it easy to resent them and we understand why. For there is so much that is urgent to do, close at hand.

But even as we do the grubby work, the patient unraveling of such problems as how to open restaurants and schools, how to give men freedom to move and think, how to make it easy to go to the polls, how to find ways of ridding employment of discrimination, how to give men the freedom to live where they can afford to live—even as we struggle with these conditions and problems, we cannot let ourselves forget what it is all "really about."

We cannot let ourselves forget—for men achieve quality only

when they keep probing depths and heights of the human situation—that we as human beings are broken and fragmented and it is our nature to be so; upon being born we are torn from certainties, separated from so much we long to unite with. This is at the essence of the human condition. But it is also at the essence of the human condition that we relate ourselves to what we are broken away from. We cannot merge, we cannot mingle, but we can relate. And it is by means of this relating, this bridging of chasms that we become new beings and learn to create a new life.

Today, I find myself thinking less of "our problem," serious as it is, and more of the whole Western way of life. Not of racial segregation alone but of all the man-made segregations in our culture. Racial segregation is, let's remind ourselves, not only a symbol of the deep, pervasive illness in our culture that has dehumanized us all. We cannot let the symptom keep us from seeing what the deeper illness really is; but because the symptom is itself a symbol, it is urgently necessary that we understand the meaning and need for the symbols.

In the first part of this essay, I mentioned symbols and facts and literal words; and the difficulty many people have in recognizing when a man's words are symbolic and when they are factual or literal.

I would like to end by returning to this matter. We know how important symbols are to men; how symbolizing was, in a sense, the means by which man became man; how man bridged the chasm between himself and other living creatures by his creative talent, his becoming a speaker and a maker. But this creativity could not have taken place had he not discovered how to use the symbol, the word that means what it literally means but also means "something else"; the thing which is actually a rag (let's say) but to a lonely child may be a relationship; that image which is an image (perhaps) of a house but a house that for someone has turned symbolically into something else, maybe all he loved in his childhood or all he hated. Our talent for symbols taught us the secret of spinning straw into gold and the more terrible secret of turning gold into straw.

We know symbolizing is a very human and most strange talent, a talent man could not have become man without. But we know, too, that though men cannot live without their symbols, those symbols must change as men change and their period in history changes and their beliefs change.

Let me remind you of the riot on the campus of the University of Georgia in 1961. Two thousand students, one night stormed the dorm where a young Negro girl—the first to enter the University—was housed. * * * They didn't know this girl, had never met her or talked with her. She was not "real" to them, she had left the earth where real people live and had gone to that mythic place in their minds where ghosts live. She had turned into a breathing symbol (and what else is a ghost?) of all they had heard about Negroes and whites in their childhood, of things they feared in their own lives, of things, perhaps, they feared or hated in women.

This riot, this stoning, was a highly symbolic occasion—far more of a rite, a primitive ceremonial, than it was an attempt to hurt or kill a "real" girl. The students had lost touch with facts, with what we call "reality" (although symbols are just as "real" on their level as a piece of wood is on its material level). But this is the important thing: *those students could have killed Charlayne Hunter. They* were in an unreal mood, yes; but Charlayne Hunter was real and the stones were real. Symbolic *acting*, except on the stage and in liturgy in church, is a dangerous business.

The heart of the matter is that the whole of our being, the whole of our lives, are affected on every level by segregation. One wonders how the "good, sane people" can accept segregation's meaning and significance without continuous inner conflict. Their facade may seem sane and even "good" but surely in order to live with themselves they must have had to become intellectually and psychically half-blind, or have had to reduce their ethical awareness to a dim point. Where is a man's quality after he has done this? The sad thing is that the quality of every one of us, however civilized we think we are, has been cheapened by the segregated life we lead.

And yet, it is not wise to let ourselves be overwhelmed with guilt. We can reduce our guilt by accepting our responsibilities. To do what? To do things and say things that will change the climate of opinion, the immediate situation. We can, as Edmond Cahn (a brilliant southerner who now practices law in New York) has said in the *Predicament of Democratic Men*, "We can prevent, we can make reparations, we can protest." But always we have to remember that there are evils, like the death of a child or a girl or a man, that we cannot make reparation for.

I would like to suggest that we can also create the new thing, or quality, the new feeling, the new relationship, the new act; and we can explore and delve and find new insight.

It may be wise to remember, also, that we cannot tear down old defenses without filling the vacuum with something else. In changing our way of life, surely it is necessary to replace what we tear down with something new and humanly valid. We create our lives, we do not solve them.

I have, during the past years, wondered about those 2,000 students in that mob at the university. I know Charlayne Hunter has grown and changed as a result of her ordeal. Have the 2,000 students changed? Have they gained insight into the reason for and the consequences of their symbolic acts that night? Have their professors helped them (in art class and literature, psychology, and philosophy) to understand what symbols and symbolic acts are, how human beings use and misuse them? Do those students now know why they abandoned the real world that fearsome night and succumbed to a symbolic acting that might have killed a girl? I hope they do. And I hope Charlayne Hunter, out of her terror, has found new insights. For I think our most creative moments come when we transform a dangerous, even disastrous situation into an opportunity for further growth and awareness. What we do with ordeal is what really counts—old wisdom, yes; but perhaps it is not amiss to remind ourselves of it.

THE ROLE OF THE POET IN
A WORLD OF DEMAGOGUES[*]

This is a sad, tragic time in the Deep South and I cannot forget it even as I say to you that tonight is a most important and pleasant occasion. For it is the anniversary of Purim, a time celebrating one of the most heroic and victorious pages of Jewish history; and it is also the birthday of that great and gentle rabbi, Dr. Stephen Wise, whose memory is beloved by all who knew him.

And too, you have chosen to honor me as a writer and woman by giving me the first Queen Esther Scroll and I would so like to tell you in person how much this moves me. But my war with cancer is, I'm afraid, somewhat like the war in Vietnam: I am into something I can't get out of right now. So—here I am: on my mountain in north Georgia, separated from you tonight.

But there are things that bring us close and it is of these I shall speak: I want to talk about the poet in a world filled with demagogues, I want to stress the power of the poetic spirit in a time of

---

[*] Acceptance speech for the first Queen Esther Scroll, awarded by the Women's Division of the American Jewish Congress, in Washington, D.C., March 17, 1965.

clamor and hate and anarchic confusion. The demagogues are everywhere: not only in Selma, Alabama, and Neshoba County, Mississippi; not only on the streets of Birmingham and Harlem and in sheriffs' offices and governors' mansions, but in the United Nations, in new countries and old, new institutions and old. Of them all, perhaps the most dangerous demagogues are those that crouch in our own minds, whispering lies at a time when we so desperately need to hear the poet's deep truths. For we have difficult problems to deal with: problems that reach inside our homes and our hearts and pull us to the ends of the earth; problems that won't leave us alone, that shock us and frighten us.

Let me name only a few: police brutality . . . Ku Klux Klan and its killers . . . capital punishment . . . drug addiction of the young . . . political tensions that grip Israel and Bonn and the Arab nations, that stir Indonesia, Vietnam, that tear at Cuba and China; there are our ghettos and our school drop-outs and our babies so bereft of love that learning is impossible; there are counties in Alabama where not one Negro has ever voted; there is the violent death of the good and valiant, Negro and white, who are trying to win dignity and freedom for others; there are the starving children of Asia; there is quiet but terrible rural depravity; there is automation—and massive conformity; always threatening us is nuclear warfare—* * *

But actually, these horrendous, multiple, interlocking problems are only aspects of one big thing: this is the vast, urgent hunger of men everywhere to become more human. *To become more human:* what could be more exalting that this amazing upsurge of the spirit, the sudden longing? The details can scare us to death, of course. But the *phenomenon as a whole* can excite us, lift us, and fill us with enormous energy and determination.

Once we see it: once we begin to realize, by act of imagination and heart, the meaning of what is happening to us, once we feel the direction we are going, then things will fall in line, chaos will resolve into new forms. And it is the poet's job to show us. For only the poet can look beyond details at the total picture; only the poet can feel the courage beyond fear, only he can grasp the splinters and bend them into a new wholeness that does not yet exist. It is *his* job to think not in years but in spans of thousands of years; *his* job to measure the slow, slow movement of the human spirit evolving; *his* to see that the moment is close for all mankind to make another big leap forward; it is *his* job to scoop up the debris of our times and show us the giant outlines of the human spirit becoming more able to relate to the unknown and the unseen.

Teilhard de Chardin was a great poet as well as a fine scientist: and, as poets often do, he now and then spoke as simply as a child. * * * In the last fifty years, he often said, more scientific problems have been articulated, more new questions asked, more discoveries made than in the past ten thousand years.

But where will all this activity take us?

It is the poets' job to tell us.

Are they doing it? What are they saying? What are novelists and dramatists saying about this tremendous thing that is happening to us? I'm afraid they are saying almost nothing. Most are still talking the old nihilisms of the nineteenth century redressed in modern clothes but the same old thing; most are still fixated on narcissistic problems that have sloshed over from Victorian days; most are still moaning about the human condition, the tragic absurdity of man's plight, the hideous lack of cosmic purpose. Most mistake an earth-size movement for no motion at all. I cannot think of one who is creating characters who might have qualities needed for this adventurous age. What has Albee given us? tiny Alice? Genet? Sartre? Mailer? "Who's Afraid of Virginia Woolf?" Albee asks: but is this really a germinal question for our times? I am afraid most cannot tear their eyes from their own small depravities. So: they are giving us fragmented sketches of sick people; they hold before us in play and story a never-ending view of miserable, most lonely schizophrenics. Of course we should look with compassion at our sick and lost ones—young and old—but they should not be presented to us in drama and novel *as though they are the whole of contemporary life,* as though they are *all we have to count on for the future.*

Turning big issues into small ones because, however talented,

they are not poet enough to grasp the vastness of contemporary possibilities;—what, really, could be more dangerous today? Turning
small issues into large. Here is where poets reduce themselves to
demagogues. By using the big distortion they become guilty of arousing needless fear and despair: they force their listeners into dead-ends
that don't exist; sealing the present tight with their own anxieties they
declare, "This age with no exit." They treat *hope* as the one, the only
four-letter word you must never be caught using.

And what effect does this have on the young? We need only to
look around: at the beats and the smokers of pot and the kids in high
school who are now drug addicts and the young homosexuals flaunting their deviations and the young heterosexuals flaunting theirs. So
few thinking in terms of the *quality* of relationships; so few yearning
to find their own secret virtue: caught like flies on sticky labels, they
stop reaching for life. These are the characters in too many of our
plays now become "real," now acting out in real homes and real
streets and real cafes the splintered fantasies the dramatists (and novelists) wrote about. Writers, poets, dramatists have forgotten what
every great artist has always known: men imitate art, art does not imitate men; everyday reality is bred from dreams, not dreams from everyday reality.

I do not want to be misunderstood: it is not the presence of splintered, sick, empty people in books and on stage that is wrong; it is the
acting *as if there is nobody else in the world;* it is the omissions, *the
absence of context,* that so dangerously distort things.

We cannot act as if this is all, as if there is nothing more to count
on; how do we dare when here we are in the midst of the greatest
transformation the human race has ever experienced! How can it be
carried through unless the young believe in it, unless they feel it IN
THE BIG! Unless they sense an exalted purpose behind this amazing
evolution of the spirit! We know man's evolution is now in his own
hands; we know from here on out it is up to him; from here on out,
he makes the decisions; he has stepped out (or God has let him step
out) of natural law—not into chaos but into a new creativity that must
find its needed forms. But do the young know this? Have the poets

offered them a new vision, a new faith, a courage that races through their blood?

It is so easy to panic, to give up in despair; it is terribly hard for poet and artist as well as for everyone else, to see around the unknown curve, to make of a handful of slivers something whole and alive, to guess by means of intuitive wisdom what the unborn thing we call our future will grow into.

But it is the great poet's job to do exactly this; and he turns into dangerous demagogue (as did Ezra Pound) when he fails his responsibilities, when he sees profound potentialities as small surface things, when he equates superficial fleeting problems with the "human condition."

But suppose the great poet does not show himself, suppose the great artist does not appear? Then it is up to you: to every sensitive person on earth to bring the poet inside himself alive. We cannot live without the poetic vision—even if we must create it ourselves, even if this means transforming our ordinary selves into creative beings. We must. For the big, dangerous problems confronting the world today are not those the scientist can handle. They are not problems that reason alone can solve; they are not amenable to statistical methods and technological instruments. These dilemmas come from our deepest roots, from the shadowy, unconscious part of our nature. Here in these depths, is the workshop of both poet and demagogue; here is where they both live and act; the poet making of amorphous uncreated material the new vision, the new excellence; the demagogue making of it the new demonology and the new perversion. And here at the heart of things you and I have our creative being, too. Your poet and demagogue—and mine—inhabit the same terrain; poet transforming, bringing new forms out of chaos, demagogue destroying. Each day, one or the other wins a small battle inside us.

Perhaps we should not leave it all to great poets and artists; perhaps this new age is challenging every one of us as *persons* to find poetic truth, to look into Orphic depths, to span with our own imagination great segments of time and space and people. Perhaps it is not only our moral natures but our creative imaginations that are being challenged today; perhaps it is the sum total of our own personal victories *as creators* that will determine what the future of mankind will be. This "perhaps" is exciting to me—and I hope, to you—for here is where we exist, here is a battle we can win and if the poet in us wins, we shall see that the human condition is not a neolithic stone [tying us] down, but a condition of continuous change taking place inside and outside the human spirit.

III

OF WOMEN,
MEN, AND
AUTOBIOGRAPHY

In Part III of this collection we are obliged to remind ourselves—more than in Parts I and II—of the historical context out of which Lillian Smith was writing. The selections in Parts I and II are clearly set against the historical reality of racism; a human problem which, although evaded, could not be denied. Because the reality of the problem has now been generally acknowledged, Smith's ideas are easy to follow, their development over time is well defined, set as they are against a tradition of racial struggle in this country, of which they form part. As a writer on race issues, Smith fits into a tradition which has clear precedent and subsequent. The selections in Part III deal primarily with the experience and difference in experience of women and men, issues which, after the earlier feminist movement in this century, had lain dormant, in a state of enforced suspended animation. Like those blacks who were called traitorous because they wanted to continue their personal struggle rather than take part, as essentially disenfranchised combatants, in World War II, women have been made to set aside their own struggle when matters of "national" importance have arisen. Additionally, the status of woman as an oppressed group has never been generally acknowledged. Lillian Smith and Paula Snelling discuss this in the first essay in this section, "Man Born of Woman," written in 1941.

The philosopher Simone Weil observed that ideas, if they are to develop into fullness, so that they can be used as something more than an intellectual parlor game, must be allowed to develop along a continuum; that once the continuum is interrupted there is a real loss. Nowhere has this been more true in Western civilization than in the female tradition. The continuum of the ideas of women has been consistently interrupted, with the result that women who choose to write about women—women like Virginia Woolf, Simone de Beauvoir, and Lillian Smith—operate not out of a naturally developed, logical intellectual past, but out of an interrupted sequence, so that their writing may seem to lack precedent and their ideas to come almost out of nowhere. We must bear this in mind as we read the work in this section.

"Man Born of Woman," which appeared in *South Today*, starts out as an investigation into the causes of war. The authors, to a certain extent, blame women for the violent nature of men, but they also recognize that women—because they are life-giving and life-preserving—are removed from and more often opposed to the phenomenon of war. The essay makes some important observations about misogyny, about the power and powerlessness of women, and about the invention of male mythology regarding women. Smith and Snelling indicate that in order for civilization to survive, women must be allowed in and made equal partners.

"Autobiography as a Dialogue between King and Corpse," a speech given at the University of Florida, May 10, 1962, was written twenty years after "Man Born of Woman." This speech repeats some of the concepts of the earlier essay, but is considerably more feminist in outlook. Smith asks the question, why have there been no great female autobiographies? Her answers are several, the most radical being that women have conspired to keep silence about themselves because to tell the truth would be to shatter the male myths about the nature of women. One such myth, which Smith explodes, is Freud's statement that women are uncivilized. Smith suggests that women are not uncivilized but that they lack loyalty to civilization. Using the disloyalty of southern women to segregation as an example—as opposed to male adherence—she states: "Instinctively woman chooses life . . . and avoids death, and she has smelled death in the word *segregation*." The second part of the speech analyzes autobiography, using as an illustration the fable from which the speech takes its title, the moral of the fable being the necessity of dealing with the many selves we all have, and depicting them, Smith says, in our autobiography.

The fragment which follows "King and Corpse" is one of the last things Lillian Smith wrote. It was her proposed beginning for her own autobiography, which she had pondered for many years but which she never lived to complete. In a note scribbled at the top of the typescript she has written: "My memoirs? Probably. The Mysteries of Autobiography as title? Perhaps."

The final speech in this section, "Woman Born of Man," given in May 1963, recounts the history of women through the identities men have bestowed on them. This is a theme which recurs in this section, it is also a theme recurrent in the literature of the women's movement. Smith mentions many of the various guises: madonna, whore, Kali, the Furies, Dante's Beatrice, Ibsen's Nora, Nabokov's Lolita, and the American housewife of the postwar years—the latter caught in the fifties trap of babies, home, PTA, car pools, etc. Smith also recounts her own history as a woman who benefited from the progress made by the suffragists and observes that the young women to whom she speaks have fewer rights than she had. In the early sixties this was not an observation made by many. The essay ends with the directive that women, for their own benefit and for the benefit of the future, seize their rights and therefore their humanity and break out of the roles in which male mythology has placed them.

The last selection in this section consists of extracts from three letters by Lillian Smith. These letters speak for themselves, about her own struggle as a woman writer who broke the silence in a closed culture. She ends the final letter with the question: "Whom, among the mighty, have I so greatly offended?"

MAN BORN OF WOMAN*

Today, with the detonation of man destroying man pounding our hearts, it is not easy to clear our minds of panic; nor easy to see the human spirit in tragic bondage to its past without being betrayed by so plain a view into despair. Yet never has a time so required of us that we keep our minds clear and our hearts quiet, as does today. For we are in deep trouble and all that we cherish is endangered. Knowing this, we must take care that we do not lose that which is most precious to us and our children.

The time has come to decide what this is, and, having once made our choice, to find ways of holding to it. And so it is that thoughtful men and women are turning away from the noise and uproar of slogans and talk of killing and being killed as solution to ills, and are searching their hearts and their minds, leafing their oldest memories as they turn the pages of history, trying to find why mankind forever seeks with evil means to bring about good and forever fails in the seeking.

* Essay in *South Today*, Winter 1941; written with Paula Snelling.

We ask ourselves questions, not expecting to find easy answers, but seeking direction in our thinking. *Do men come together in order that they may more abundantly create, or more effectively destroy? For what they can give each other, or for what they can help each other take from outsiders? When men combine to kill other men, do they do so as a means to an end or as end in itself? If war was once necessary as a method for getting food and security, is it still unavoidable for the same reason? If the avowed purposes which mass-murder subserves can be attained by other processes, are we willing to relinquish it or do we crave it for its own sake? If it is dear to us even when it does not bring us material gains, or when other technics are available by which those same gains can be had, is it yet possible for us to renounce it? If we are unwilling or unable to do so, what alternative awaits us?*

Each chapter of history, from earliest to latest page, shows man hunting in packs to kill his kind. One may seek the genesis of this trait in speculations concerning prehistoric brothers, banished by a jealous father, banding together to depose the tyrant and put a bloody end to his monopoly of female society, or may content oneself with punier, more orthodox hypotheses. But the fact remains indisputable; and points us to the necessity of inquiring—though only briefly here—into the functions of groups and the economics on which their stability depends as we search for rational ways of meeting the world's urgent needs.

In earlier days there was no great dichotomy between the individual and his group: they stood to profit by the same success. But gradually through centuries, their paths have diverged. The individual, with missteps and fumblings, has repressed some of those infantile and savage desires which once were the mainsprings of his actions. He has come really to want many of the civilized and humane things which at first he only thought he ought to want, and later wished he wanted; but now he actually wants them, and to limited but perceptible degree, has attained them. Meanwhile the "group"—in the beginning an instrument by which the individual got what he wanted when not strong enough alone to get it—has come to have varied and complex functions, some of which now imperil its members.

Though force was once necessary in order to wrest a living from the earth and its creatures, we have at last created potentialities for producing and distributing goods sufficient for the world's needs so that today it would seem that, at rational levels, only avarice and inertia require man to resort to the inflicting of death in order to obtain materials of living. At the same time that these pressures have let up so that they no longer necessitate war, other internal and external conditions have arisen which make continued resort to it suicidal. And with tools perfected to the point where man can wipe himself off the map any day he chooses, knowledge that he may do so burdens humanity with deep anxiety.

Could we but view our peril sanely and utilize our resources for averting it, there would be less need for panic. For the psychologists and social scientists have been as busy during recent decades as have inventors of machines. True—so long as we do not act constructively on it, the knowledge they bring us of the submerged, unflattering psychic motivations which propel us to war, of the scope and needlessness of human misery, of the inadequacy and insanity of mass-murder as solution for social ills only adds to our nervous tension. But this knowledge, in the hands of those having more fundamental allegiance to life than to death, to truth than to hypocrisy, to justice than to greed, could transform the world.

Through the generations there have been men who have striven valiantly toward this end but they have been too few for the magnitude of the task. And woman, taking herself at man's valuation, has kept hands off. (Which may or may not have been justifiable in the days when his capacity to kill was only a fraction of her capacity to reproduce. But the ratio is rapidly reversing itself and she can no longer afford indifference to this male group-trait which threatens the race.)

In seeking reasons why man in his group activities responds with warmth to mastery of the tools for destruction and coolness to utilization of the machinery for social betterment, we must bear in mind that the scales are weighted to that end. For the individual's constructive impulses are each free to find full immediate outlet in small solitary acts; whereas his destructive impulses are so far as possible held in check—dammed up to form a reservoir of cumulative power which the individual alone dares not take responsibility for letting loose. With the result that, when the group-conscience at intervals sanctions concerted outlet for it, each individual is propelled into the channel with a force many times greater than is at any moment accumulated within him for creative deeds. Another reason why destructive acts come easier to the group than do constructive acts is that formerly concerted aggression was necessary: men were so many, and available goods so few, that only those who banded themselves together in the most effectively destructive group lived to propagate their talents. And their sons who through countless generations found group violence indispensable for survival are loath now to relinquish it even though under the changed circumstances of today it holds as great threat to its users as to their adversaries. For man (who created not life, but the intricate machinery of civilizaton and the devious patterns by which it is maintained) cherishes *his* creation in all its manifestations and is as loath to destroy even its most hideous malformations as woman is to destroy an imbecile child to whom she has given birth. This tenacious conservatism becomes another obstacle to rational progression toward peace. As does the fact, which we tend to discount, that from ancient times war has been a psychic release for those cultural renunciations of cannibalism and murder which society early required of its individuals. Making these demands when its own existence was imperiled by their continuance, it succeeded in imposing these sacrifices upon individuals only by inaugurating ceremonials in which the group periodically performed as rites those very acts prohibited its members separately, and by giving value received in some form of emotional satisfaction not otherwise available to them, thus deeply entrenching war among peoples not only for the direct emotional and material satisfactions it gives but because it was the plausible surrogate, the public festival, the orgy by which the group recompensed its members for day by day denials of their impulses. A more obvious hindrance in modern times to peaceful settlement of difficulties is the individual's hunger for power and his efforts to satisfy it by identifications with powerful groups—a phenomenon we are having to consider increasingly in a mechanized culture where individuals function more and more as cogs.

But in discussions of war, the bitter and ancient dilemma of "man born of woman," its sharpening of his hunger for power, its intensifying of his stubborn holding to old patterns, is too little dwelt upon. In war as in peace, in civilization's destruction as in its creation, cherchez la femme is of eternal relevance. Man's humiliation at her hand has been monstrous and her tyranny a dread thing to endure. It has been sensible of him that he learned long ago to turn his hate and fear of her, equalling his injury but rarely cancelling out his love, against the first distant object concerning which he could make a grudge; and it is only natural that he now cling to this archaic pack-hunting habit to escape her!

(Perhaps it is not too trivial to note here that woman with her sharp, unmoral tongue has never invented vituperatives against the male to equal his abusive words having her for target;—a mere *hellion-bitch-whore* heating the mind with their connotations. Nor to recall that man in anger tells off man, not by direct, searing blasts of profanity but by reminding him in bitter circuitousness that he is the son of this, that, the other cursed female. Such fury and hate so philologically cast in woman's image is not wisely ignored by those who search the past for the whys of our world-wide trouble and the future for its solution. One smiles in the saying of it. Yet something in each man and woman acknowledges its truth.)

If man dared to thrust into the open his unending secret enmity against woman, there might be less of nation warring with nation; less need for him to merge his longing for superiority into a great mass-lust for power, less need for him to find outlet for his hate— drives which so complicate the more simple and rational needs of peoples. Pressures of population, of trade, of control of basic resources, now so compelling would recede in size and strength to the point where he might conceivably deal rationally with them. For in a world where there is abundance for all, these are practical matters requiring only that special intelligence and skill in organizing production and devising distribution with which man is so highly endowed. How different might be the problems which confront us with such hideous stubbornness today had not man been forced to find diversion from his ancient and bitter duel with woman by projecting his hostility and jealousy of her upon antagonists with whom he has a reasonable chance of victory!

And yet how could he have done otherwise? For the only overt group act of aggression (though sabotage never ceases) which he can commit against her—who, calling forth his hate as mother-sister-wife-daughter is yet because of these tender relationships inviolate to his or his clan's attack—is to smother her firmly with the sacerdotal robes of "sacred womanhood," and push her with gentle but exceedingly determined hand out of his man's world and back into place on her pedestal—segregating her as he does all groups without organized power, who threaten his supremacy in this his self-made civilization. Segregating her, putting her always and forever in her "place" . . . Man the victor each day she invades his civilization; man the vanquished each night he returns to the home, where he was born, where he learned all that he knows of tenderness and security and life, and yet where he tries so desperately—not to die. As if for her, who has borne him, suckled him, diapered him, to shroud him is more than his strained dignity can bear . . .

To get at the genesis of the ancient trouble between man and his woman we tell a fable, though it is a little wryly that we once more remind him of his humble beginnings:

In her body woman carried man for nine months. For nine months he was dependent upon her and secure and satisfied in his dependence with a completeness so near perfection in a world of desolating imperfections that out of this blissful experience must have sprung all his later dreams of a Utopian world . . . and his insatiable hunger for that nearest approximation to this early state he is ever likely to attain: death.

And though a time came when he was thrust out into a world not so warm, not so comfortable, yet for a while he was with reassuring frequency granted respites—ecstatic reunions with her from whom he had been so abruptly parted. Suckling her breast, filling his body with her strength, gave him confirmation of his old dream—and perhaps the first desire to destroy the source of this dream . . .

But going on: a time comes when there are no more of these moments. He is admonished to be a little man; to be big and strong "like your father." And he looks up at father and sees in magnificently enlarged proportions someone who resembles too much—himself. And though he trembles with awe and gazes in vague admiration at this god (or devil) responding to stark power of size, seeing in these heroic dimensions his own future self, he remains yet doubtful for he also remembers with somatic urgency that once he was very small, and to be so small was good—as nothing in life since has ever been good.

The little boy continues to grow . . . hungering at times to attain the giant size of this hero the woman has urged him to become. She admires bigness. She too seems so awed by the magnificent physical power of "father" that she lets her own body grow humble and complaisant and makes of it a willing goal for father's exploring energies. She *lets* father—

Ah . . . if the little boy had never perceived this! For in realizing this he guesses the woman's terrible strength and grows afraid. For he sees that in cunning she adorns herself with weakness. He sees, yet cannot believe his own eyes, that she adds stature to her victim by the simple act of looking high above his head, until, following her eyes, he towers above her in satisfying superiority. Then, as if absentmindedly, she pulls his head gently into her lap, smoothes his curls, gathers them suddenly into her sure fingers and snips them off—reducing her victim to his old role of small boy. But when man's humiliation has grown unbearable, her eyes once more wander skyward, and following her gaze he is again looking down upon her . . . and now feeling his strength he strides forth to confirm it, he goes out to conquer all the evil worlds that ever there have been, and in the going, he attains great and awesome height; but to her eyes, as she waves him on his valiant path, he still casts only a small boy's shadow behind him, and it is well that he does not turn back to see . . .

After a time the little boy too is grown. And he goes about among the women, trying his strength with them, loving and fearing the mother in every creature he meets . . . and his hate grows as he recognizes in each of them the old cunning weakness of her, the earth's strong creature. But in desperation he takes one of them to mate— having no other choice.

And after a vague time his woman brings forth a child. *How did you do that?* he demands. *I don't know,* she says, bewildered by such a question. *But you must know!* he cries in sudden male envy, *you must! How could you have done it if you don't know?* And woman stares at her mate a moment, then thrusts the baby into his arms. *But it is here,* she whispers, *that's all that matters, dear, isn't it, it's here!* And he jealously looks down at his woman's handiwork, gulps doggedly, *You ought to know how you did it. You ought to know! It's the only thing,* he mutters brokenly, *that does matter—the way it was done. You're just a woman,* he adds in loud sudden scorn, *that's what! Nobody but a woman could think a little red-faced squirming result as important as the way!* And he bangs the door in her puzzled face, strides out into the woods and squatting there on a rock in utter loneliness he lets his heart fill with misery. But after a while, he feels something slowly stir in his mind, and lo, it begins to grow, and his mind stretches full with it until its growth is complete . . . and now in great excitement he takes *his* creation to the house, he calls her, *See,* he shouts proudly, *see what I've done!* But woman cannot see. *You must see,* he cries angrily, *it's here before your eyes! You've got to see; It has a name,* he whispers, *Logic I call it,* and flushed with pride. *Oh that!* woman says and hurries back to the baby. *Did you think that something real, dear? That's just a way, not always the best way either, real things are made, sometimes.*

Time passes. Man goes about his living. And each time his woman grows big with child he turns morose, confronted thus baldly with his ineptitude. And when it comes forth he in shame observes that she with simple ease offers it nourishment which he with all his prowess and daring could not give.

But little by little, with logic's bright eyes to help (whom loyally he never abandons) the puzzle is pieced together until the Way grows brilliantly clear and he is filled with arrogant triumph and importance, knowing now that woman with all her assurance is as nothing without him. Then one day he hears a crackle in the woods, sees a shadow go past . . . and ugly suspicion clouds his certainty. And when next she calls him to come see what she has to show him, he stands before her moodily, suddenly asking with abrupt sharpness if it is his own. *Of course dear!* she murmurs. *How silly!* she muses, and smiles as she draws him down to her breast, *who else's could it be?*

The fable has no end . . . But one cons it, wondering in profound seriousness if some melioration of the discord between man and woman is not prerequisite to enduring peace between nations. It was this ancient warfare between the sexes that drove man, self-exiled from a simple home, into housing himself with a fantastically complex civilization—a civilization whose brilliance and versatility critics of our modern age sometimes do not give sufficient credit to. Yet his great skill in organizing complex groups and institutions, his almost fantastic talent for getting things done if he wants them done, make it even more difficult, if one considers rational causes only, to understand his utter failure to erect the machinery for internationalism and peace. And if woman's protestations of hating war and loving peace are sincere, then surely the time has come on this unhappy earth for her to seek out and face if she can the deep-lying forces which impel man on his road to destruction of the civilization he has so proudly erected.

Looking about, we find her past aloofness from civilization, though it may have contributed heavily to its threatened fall, also fits her peculiarly for its saving. Through heritage and generations of habit she differs in pertinent respects from men. Her sins—and they are many—she has committed singly, not in herds. Her acts both good and evil have taken place because she, or someone she personally loved or hated, wanted or did not want them to take place, not in the service of an abstraction or under group-hypnosis. The compulsion to be one of the crowd is not an integral part of female psychology. (When women appear similarly garbed on Easter and other mornings, it is not with that intent, but because they are equally handicapped and equally ingenious in carrying through the urge to be better dressed than the others.) It requires no great psychic effort for them to resist the magnetic pull of the group, for they have never been under its domain. Women do not have the age-old undertow of group loyalty to combat which would impel them to stand together right or wrong, and to rationalize their acts; nor have they as much thirst to merge themselves with the group in sensuous enjoyment of its pervasive erotic attraction (both of which male characteristics may have their origin in those banished-brothers days). And even if it be true that women hate no less than men, are impelled no less than they to destroy, are no more inclined to turn their destructive impulses inward, still they would be less likely to choose war as a solution; for they are less given to symbolism, *less likely to be satisfied with killing the wrong person.*

But there are reasons for thinking that woman does not share equally man's affinity for death. If it be true, as some philosophers assert, that death is an integral part of life, not something superimposed upon it (if organic matter carries with it, inextricably, the seeds of its own destruction), it is probably also true that among the polarities of the universe, masculinity and death, femaleness and life, are linked together. And by simple mathematics, qualitative differences to one side, the sex which has to spend nine months in the begetting of each human being would have less time to devote to the service of death, were it equally inclined, than has the sex of whom nine minutes are required. Add to that the thirty years during which by custom woman is harnessed to the cradle, caught in the treadmill of the home, and one sees that, whatever her impulses, she could not have made of herself the effective bondservant of death which man has become.

While through the generations woman has borne, nurtured, and conditioned for better and for worse the raw material of humanity, she has contributed little else toward civilization. The group life of the race has been, directly, a creation of man. Whether through the fortuitousness of circumstances or because of inherent differences between the sexes, the evils which characterize mass activities are perhaps too deeply inbred now in the male for him alone to save the race from their accelerating effects. Although it is doubtful that civilization could have come into being without the concomitant of violence, the callousness to life, the sacrifice of tree to forest which man in his allegiance to abstraction has incorporated into his soul, it is equally doubtful that civilization in its present state can endure, and preserve its beneficent qualities, without a more drastic curbing and uprooting of those same tendencies than man alone can inaugurate and carry through. And woman, who thus far has been permitted to enjoy parasitically the benefits of civilization, will perish with her host unless she can aid him in liberating himself from his seductor death.

But her task will be three-fold and difficult. And remembering her past, one is none too confident of her success, notwithstanding her special qualifications.

For ten thousand years civilized woman's major job has been that of mother. As a brooder she has done her work honorably—measuring up well to the efficient gestation standards of female animals. But as a mother of human children she has learned little during the centuries. She has not acquired, nor made effort to acquire, even moderate skill in guiding her child up the steep stairs of those emotional attachments along which he must pass on his way to psychic maturity, but instead with compulsive repetitiousness she attempts again and again to tie the severed umbilical cord to herself, holding him desperately to his infantilism. Indifferent or blind to frustrations piling higher and higher in his heart as he moves from year to year of his life, she implacably urges the little savage to make those rigorous cultural renunciations which our civilization requires of everyone entering it and yet gives no heed to how he shall be recompensed for his painful sacrifices.

It is an indictment of woman in her role of mother that millions upon millions of her sons today turn to war and violence as the "way out" of their deep trouble, some eager to give vent to those destructive feelings which she has cultivated assiduously through her blindness and stupidity and narcissistic urges; others, hating violence but perplexed by desires too ambivalent for rational choice, reluctantly following the old familiar way of bloodshed . . .

It is an indictment of her that it was left to man to discover all the knowledge that we have of childhood. For not only has she failed in her role of mother but she has used it as an excuse for her empty mind. She has taken pride in her obscurantism. Despite her great talent for plumbing her man's heart, she understands little of her own; despite her ability to look at the world realistically without the blinders of man's romanticism, she does not value the knowledge she thus gains and makes no effort to acquire more by a discipline of her mind. In her primary job of child-rearing she has relied, not upon knowledge but with narcissistic complacency she has preferred to believe that *her* child's nine months' intra-uterine existence guaranteed its future welfare. With primitive, dumb assurance she has for ten thousand years believed, despite glaring evidence to the contrary, that because her body somehow brought the little germ cell to fruition, she with no further intellectual effort understands the complexities of the civilization for which she prepares her child, comprehends the intricate and subtle processes of his infantile emotional development, and is divinely equipped to nurture and guide him as is no other. It is no wonder that a great man like Sigmund Freud, who taught the world almost all it knows about the child's emotions, spoke of woman a little contemptuously as "culturally stunted."

We can hardly forget these things when we urge woman to go forth as saviour of a weary, sinning race of men. We grow uncertain remembering her regressive mind-set, remembering the narrow circumference of her love and her loyalty as we face an unknown future which seems to be leading toward a form of internationalism, to be shaping itself blindly and awkwardly but inevitably into a democratic world order for which not only new technics and new institutions will be needed but expanding imagination and loyalties which can encompass the whole of mankind as securely, as warmly as woman's body encloses the life of her son.

In extenuation of our sex's sins, we remember that we are an oppressed group, that man put our mind in prison. But we have grown to love our chains. We have learned to exploit, as do other minority groups, our "weakness" (that poor lie which man so defensively labeled his woman with!). And yet, forsaking a direction which is leading us straight into a dead-end of despair, we now change direction (in that way so exasperating to the male) and say again that unless woman *does* make this tremendous effort, disaster can hardly be avoided for her children. Knowing the strength of her primitive, animal life instinct, somehow we believe, despite her sloth, that she will summon the will to hold on tenaciously and once more give value to the living in a world where life is now held so cheap.

But her task will be difficult. In her home she must use the knowledge which psychoanalysis offers her to level her own and her family's mounting frustrations, to gain understanding of human needs and ways of fulfilling them, to find outlets in creative directions for destructive urges, using hate as manure, to make green fields for living children—not cemeteries for dead sons. She must, in addition, learn again the ancient ways of the female, the subtle strengths of her sex—birthrights she has sold for the pottage of a specious "equality" in man's world. Not that she must retire from his world (as Hitler and others suggest, perceiving, though crudely, some of man's basic trouble) but rather bring with her into it as substitutes for a competitor's tricks—the old wisdom and versatility which if understood by her and used with scruple would enable her to play with brilliant virtuosity the complex, modern role of mother-companion-lover. How chivalrously woman could acknowledge man's great achievements in the fabulous world he has made for himself, knowing it was she who drove him into it, out of the home. How graciously she should insist upon no belittling of his proved superiority of mind and muscle, armed as she is by nature with such lethal weapons! Yet instead of the magnificent role that could be hers, instead of the comfort and security which she could with bland tenderness give a world sorely in need today, she cheaply and treacherously vacillates between the sinuous acts of Delilah and the parasitic ways of a child; she denies her own femaleness by assuming the less attractive aspect of the male; or else betrays man by bestowing the love that is rightfully his upon his sons . . . She must learn again the ancient lesson which will teach her that however swiftly the old way goes and the new way comes, man's dreams of himself will never change.

Less difficult surely, yet demanding persistence and effort, she must learn to live as a civilized, humane, informed world-citizen, refusing (for her home has no wall around it that will protect it from aerial bombs) narrow provincialisms of thought and feeling, remembering that she has let her love through too many uncounted centuries carry her across the enemy's lines into his arms, for her now to deem insurmountable the historic and arbitrary boundaries of race, of nation, of class on a globe already shrunk so small by radio, and airplane and interlocking needs as to make anachronistic and suicidal all artificial barriers to human relations.

Autobiography as a Dialogue
between King and Corpse*

We have no record that Adam was aware of himself before Eve gave him that first long look. She was his primal mirror. It must have been quite a shock to discover himself in a female's eyes. Yet this profoundly traumatic experience has not been dealt with adequately either in poetry or psychology.

Freud missed it entirely—as he missed so much that is important about women and men and their relationship with each other. I cannot remember that Jung has said anything remarkable about this archetypal experience. Ferenczi wrote a book called *Thalassa* which is full of wonderful symbols and poetic half-truths, but one would hardly say it is about this subject of self-awareness. It is basically a book about a room with one exit, or we might call it, the biological point of no return. Ferenczi's idea was that the infant human being liked his first small room, left it under passionate protest and has longed, ever since, to return to it. But while this nostalgia for the womb is hypnotic stuff, and has a great deal to do with men's love of

* Speech at the University of Florida, May 10, 1962.

the sea and ships, and with Western men's quest, and with *Moby Dick*, it has little to do with women as mirrors.

The women, themselves, have never written much about what Eve saw when she looked at Adam, although what she saw may have had a great deal to do with her learning to talk, first. She has whispered about it to other women for a million years, and some of what she whispered has leaked out, of course.

What is more important—at least, to our topic of autobiography—is the fact that women have not broken the million-year silence about *themselves*. Or, they are only beginning to. They know how *they* look in men's eyes. At least, they should. For poetry and art and myth and fiction and religion are filled with icons and images and dreams and nightmares about the female; and there are the Greek furies and maenads and the Protestant witches, and the Catholic Madonna and always King Arthur's Court, et cetera.

But they dare not record how they look to themselves. Why?

There are reasons. One is: there are many women who have no awareness of themselves. They have never asked who they are and they don't care. And there are the appeasers, who may have their own ideas, but have settled, publicly, for the men's view. It seems the simplest way to live and often the only way to keep the bread buttered. There are others, confused by what they have been told which is not in the least what they know about themselves, who have settled things by turning off the light in their interiors; they are different and they know it but these differences are easier to accept if unnamed.

But there is a more cogent reason why women have kept their silence. They dare not tell the truth about themselves for it might radically change male psychology. And this change might prove more upsetting to the world than even the cold war nations playing ball with nuclear bombs. How do we *know* what might happen?

So—playing it safe—women have conspired to keep their secrets.

Recently, Dorothy Baker wrote a small book called *Cassandra at the Wedding*. It is, as far as I know, the most candid and perceptive account ever printed of girls and women and their feelings for each other and themselves. It is also very funny. An advance copy came to me. I read it; and purring like a tabby cat on a warm hearth, I waited to see what the men would do with it. I put up a small bet with friends that this book would not be given women to review. And it wasn't—certainly for the most part. I shall not take time here to tell you what the men said. But I suggest you read the book. Then go back and read those reviews.

But great autobiographies are not written by people who have conspired to keep silent, and we must face the fact that no woman has yet written a great autobiography.

However, women are exceptionally good at memoirs and diaries and journals. They rarely tell the truth, even in their diaries, about their sex experiences or their most intimate relationships; nor do they spend much time asking the unanswerable questions about the meaning of human life since they have never been too sure they were human. But they have a blunt, and highly entertaining way of cutting the homefolks down to size; they see the specific things, the small events that are so often full of heart-stopping implications; and they can get it on paper. As you know, the best women writers do not use a self-conscious literary style but write the spoken language with beautiful precision, and sometimes with poetic lyricism.

This down-to-earth, vivid, and sometimes poetic quality in their writing has a certain enchantment. We all know women are less given to abstractions and generalities than are men—not because they are not capable of abstract and categorical thinking but because they are, like artists, closer to things, to the human flesh, and human feelings; and they tend to remember that the concrete is always different while the abstract has a deadly sameness. And because they avoid abstractions, it follows that they tend to be less romantic than men. Maybe much of it comes from their age-old task of changing diapers and washing them; laying out the dead (in old days), giving medicine and enemas, doing the homey, dirty, naked sort of things that only women and doctors and today's undertakers are familiar with.

This earthy contact with flesh makes for vividness but it tends to strip the glamor off of things. Not long ago, a famous American politician was being honored in a big city. The streets were filled with hundreds of thousands of people; the flags were out; the bands were playing; office workers were dropping the usual strips of paper from high-up windows. Here came the bubble-top car, the motorcycles, the rush, the gasp; and the big hurrah. Then a woman in the crowd turned to those near her and said, "Bless him, I put his first diaper on him." Now any astute politician would avoid that woman as if she had the plague. How could he convince himself, after such a deflating encounter, that he could be president or secretary of state or even justice of the peace!

Women, including women writers, have this tendency to deflate the hero's ego. But, even though it is hard to forgive them this sin, we must admit that in their diaries and journals they have left us some unforgettable pages. What women are more different from each other than Harriet Martineau, Virginia Woolf, Dorothy Wordsworth—yet they all have given us in letters or diaries a superb unforgettable awareness of fragments of the human experience. Even their rebellion [has for me] a special poignancy. I find myself thinking of Virginia Woolf's A *Room of One's Own*. It was an outburst—and her men friends were cool to her, afterward, for weeks—it was an impassioned protest of women's position in the world, of the woman writer's almost insuperable difficulties. It is certainly not her best writing. Nor does it reveal her most interesting and subtle qualities as a woman. Yet it sticks with you. Such plain, raw facts, so deeply felt by one woman and so meaningful to millions of others!

Women have been particularly good with the bitter times of war. They push aside the politicians and the speeches, the war cries and the jingoism and write about things as they exist in the home or town or in their small group of friends. Men have often accused women of not having the imagination to see things in the big; and I do think women may care less about extending the periphery of their awareness, and more about deepening it. However that may be, women who write about wars concern themselves with the personal. It is the torn relationship that counts, the sudden break-off of small futures, the house that falls in on itself. Statistical thinking is impossible; Patriotism is an abstraction and women are quick to hear its spurious jangling. Vera Brittain in her *Testament of Youth*—which was meaningful to my generation after the First World War—caught the full poignancy of the death of the young, the tearing up of lives that were only beginning. She told us of a million young men by telling us of three or four whom she loved; she caught the universal by holding fast to the individual and special sorrow. The book was an impassioned cry from the heart. Yet, so vividly and concretely did she catch the ten thousand small personal events that made up her life during those years, that it stands now, fresh and clear. Vera Brittain has brilliant intellectual equipment—as have many women writers—but with the intuition of an artist, she uses this equipment only to keep her firmly oriented and relies on her eye, ear, heart, memory to do the real job.

The women who kept diaries in the Civil War are the ones who have given us the most reliable pictures of those times. They recorded our individual differences while the newspapers recorded our group samenesses. Freud said once that woman is not well acculturated; she is, he stressed, retarded as a civilized person. I think what he mistook for her lack of civilization is woman's lack of *loyalty* to civilization. Southern women have never been as loyal to the ideology of race and segregation as have southern men. The southern woman has always put the welfare of one individual above the collective welfare or collective values. Many of them have been betraying White Supremacy for two hundred years but most who have done so could not reason with you as to why. Instinctively woman chooses life, wherever life is, and avoids death, and she has smelled the death in the word *segregation*. I am sure that in totalitarian countries there have been all along many women who have decided their acts not by the public ideology but by each day's personal equation.

But, though we were given many letters and diaries that tell us how *unsolid* the South was even the year before the war began, how torn were the hearts and minds and souls of men and women, there did not come out of this traumatic ordeal one good autobiography. The southern woman played it by ear, day by day—and never, afterward, turned back to see what significance, what meaning, lay in what she had actually done and said and thought, and recorded. She could not form a *gestalt* and say: *This has been my life and my people's life.* The Reconstruction was not good psychological soil for contemplation or self-criticism, for men or women. Ordeal can become so heavy a thing that the individual, in his anxiety, merges with the collective self and region and loses his own identity. Of all the sad results of the South's long drawn out and unresolved ordeal, this, to me, has been the most tragic: that even the writers of the South could not hold on to their own Self, could not find out who they were, and settled for being merely white southerners. In their anxiety and confusion, they finally killed their own personal dreams and settled for singing hymns to the collective dream of the region; they forgot the myths of the human race and settled for one pseudo-myth which was no more than a pitiful fantasy.

With all their talent for the specific and concrete, with their capacity for passion and for disloyalty to conformity, women have not, as yet, written autobiographies that deserve the word "great."

Have men? Yes. Yes—and no. But may I come back to this later?

For I should like now to tell you the story of the king and the corpse—an old Hindu tale which in recent years has been elegantly retold by Heinrich Zimmer. You may know it. If so, perhaps you do not mind my giving a brief resume:

There was once a good king. An intelligent king who felt he had the necessary kingly qualities of sympathy, responsibility, energy, courage, and a well-informed mind. He also thought he was wise. Until one day, a holy man, a sadhu, came to his audience room and silently proffered him a piece of fruit which the king carelessly accepted and handed to his treasurer who stood behind him. Once each year, the holy man came with his gift. And each time, it was received casually and handed in silence to the treasurer.

Until the tenth year: It happened that the king's concubine's monkey was sitting on his shoulder that day when the holy man proffered the fruit and the monkey grabbed it and began to eat it. At the center of the fruit was a jewel of great value which fell to the floor. You can guess what happened next: The treasurer picked it up then dashed to the porch of the treasure house where he had carelessly thrown the rest of the fruit; there on the floor, amidst mold and rot, were nine jewels of priceless value. The king, being generous, gave the jewels to the treasurer. Then he turned and asked the holy man if he wished to speak with him. The holy man told him that great courage would be required for a venture he would like to tell the king about privately, but it was an important venture and needed a king's courage. Would the king help him? The king said he would.

He was then told to go, on a certain night, to the burial ground outside the city, where thieves and murderers and other criminals were executed and cremated. The king duly arrived on the specified night. The place was full of corpses, ghouls, smoke, smells, and ghostly howls. It wasn't a pleasant place. The beggar ascetic was waiting.

"Now," said the man who pretended he was holy, "go across the grounds and you will find a corpse hanging on a tree. Cut it down and bring it to me." The king went to the tree and found the corpse; he climbed the tree, cut the corpse down and hoisted it up on his back. He was walking along when the corpse groaned. The king, thinking he was imagining things, laughed; and the corpse hopped off his back and went back and hung himself on the tree.

Once more, the king cut him down; once more put him on his back. He was silent this time, as he walked along. Then a voice from the corpse said, "Perhaps it would entertain you, on your journey if I were to tell you a story." He proceeded to do so. The story had to do with the right and wrong acts of several people which had resulted in the death of two innocent people. The corpse said, "Tell me who was responsible for the old people's death. If you know you must tell me or your head will burst in a hundred pieces."

The king thought a moment and gave the spectre a most judicious answer, saying the king of that realm was really responsible for the goings-on of his subjects for he should be the all-seeing eye, the father of his subjects. The corpse hopped off his back and ran to the tree and hung himself on it again.

Twenty-four times, the spectre told a story and asked a question; and twenty-four times the king with much thoughtfulness answered the spectre as to who were the ones responsible for what had occurred. But after the twenty-fifth story, the king could not find an answer. He said, "It is all very confused; each is so involved with the other that I cannot separate them and their acts, nor can I name their relationships for what they are."

"Ah . . ." said the spectre, "I shall leave you now; take the corpse to the holy man. But listen: he is not a holy man; he practices black magic and delves into dark, evil places; do not confuse this with holiness. He is going to lure you to a magic circle and once you are there, he will induce you to worship *me* whom he will try to put back into the corpse. But you do this and that"—and he outlined the tricks— "and you can destroy him instead of his destroying you." All he was told to do the king manfully did. And was, henceforth, freed of this magic, superstitious self—for it was that—which had tended to drag him back to the black magic and other dangerous practices. Practices which are open to the human being but which will, if indulged in, destroy him.

Those twenty-five stories are wiser and more challenging than anything I can say to you here. Read them for yourself. Were they dreams? Maybe. Our dreams are as important as the more obvious realities. Whatever they mean, these stories have endured for thousands of years; and have been used by artists and story tellers again and again—among them Thomas Mann.

But what does this have to do with autobiography? Everything. Each of us tells ourselves at least twenty-five stories about our own life; and tries to answer the questions that arise from them; but wisdom comes only when we recognize that there are questions that cannot be answered, and selves within us which we have created that must be recognized and then rendered harmless to us.

A man, writing his autobiography, tends to choose one self and tell only that self's story. And sometimes it is worth telling; sometimes not. The monkey, who is one of our playful, irresponsible selves, will see and devour the sweet fruit of life and carelessly throw away the precious gems at the center. There are writers who tell us only the monkey's story—as did Henry Miller in *The Tropic of Cancer*. He has, since then, given us some jewels. Others tell us—and this is especially true of those in public life—of the king's story. Winston Churchill's autobiographical writings have been a monologue which the king held with himself. That does not mean it is worthless, even though he has told us little about his other selves. We can dimly see the monkey on his shoulders, and the monkey in pantomime tells us more, perhaps, than Mr. Churchill has any idea of. But his other selves? Do we glimpse the holy man who is not holy at all? Do we hear the spectre which each man creates within himself asking Mr. Churchill questions? Does Mr. Churchill answer them all—or does he finally say, as did the wise king, "This I do not understand; this is a place where evil and good, right and wrong are so braided together that I cannot disentangle them."

To write the perfect autobiography would of course require a man able to accept and bring all his selves together; one who has reached down into the depths and wandered through the human race's burial ground, and there talked with the spectre who, in turn, has talked with death; and at the same time he would need to be the king who has played a responsible, intelligent role in the public and semipublic life of his times. This man would need to take his past and find the exact point where it joins his future; he would need to know the archaic depths of the unconscious and at the same time criticize these depths with a rational, logical mind; he would need to accept and understand his childhood as well as his present; and he would, finally, need to be a man who knows a great story never gives an answer to its listeners but instead asks a great question. I have for years been asking myself, When is a story a real story? The only satisfying answer I have found is this: When a story begins with one specific question about life or even a handful of questions and ends with a bigger question, one that human beings must keep asking, knowing as they ask that it cannot be answered, then a story is a real story—and maybe an immortal one.

So: when a story teller—and every autobiographer is a story

teller—starts out to tell his own story, he has to search deep and wide to know what that story really is. This is a spiritual and intellectual ordeal. It is more: it is a creative ordeal, for he is actually creating his own Self and his own life as he writes, because he is giving it its meaning. Let us say that he spends two, three, four, or ten years on this writing venture: all of this time, he is exploring, searching for the basic pattern, knowing it is there (for it is always there); searching, too, for that little one-act play which begins to act itself out almost in babyhood and continues until death. What self is this that must enact and reenact a little one-act play? Is it a valid self? Should it be included in our autobiography? Can we relate it to the monkey and the king and the spectre and the spurious holy man, and the religious suppliant and, maybe, to the princess, and the queen?

What a courageous, and almost demi-urgic task to set out on the quest for the meaning of one's life, what stoical honesty is required in order to set it down!

No wonder most of us settle for smaller matters. No wonder women for the most part have settled for notebooks and diaries and journals—as have some of our great male writers: Gide, for instance, and Dostoevski in his Underground notes. There have been others who settled for the king in themselves—as Churchill did; as many artists have done—and in doing so, they have told us much about politics, and much about art. Others have settled for one period in their lives: their childhood, or their teenage experiences. Or perhaps, as some women have been recently doing well, their experiences with their mothers or fathers. Others—the greatest of whom may be St. Augustine, although several of the Catholic saints must be included alongside him—have concentrated on their relationship with God. Kierkegaard did this—and his writings say much to us, today, in our torn, anguishing fragmentations: our struggles between science with its small answers and religion with its great questions.

I hope, some day, to write my autobiography. I have not yet done so—although most of my writing is autobiographical. In one book, *Killers of the Dream*, I have chosen to take one fragment of my life, my experiences as a white person in a strictly patterned highly conformed culture, and write as fully as I could of that. I have told in that book many true things about my childhood as I lived it and my brothers and sisters lived it and my friends lived it—and strangers I did not know, lived it. Only in a tight, closed culture could such a book be written. A German, reared as a child in the Nazi days, could give us a book of similar worth. Why did I do this—instead of writing about myself as an individual? Because I was not a free individual during some of those years, I was a white conformist. I told both as documentary and as confession my story as one human being caught in the white-black strands of a web that seemed to be soft and pliable but was made of thin steel wires which caught and held and wounded the human spirit.

Someone asked me, "Did you write this book as an act of penance?" I think, perhaps, I did in a way—as every autobiography is an act of penance; but it was also, for me, if I may say a very serious thing, a step toward redemption. As was St. Augustine's *Confessions*. I began the book not to give answers but to find the big questions that I could and must live with in freedom. And because the situation I lived in, and still live in, is one of great importance to the earth's future, because segregation as I knew it and others in the South knew it is both symbol and symptom of the deep malaise which the human race is suffering from, I also appealed in this book to the reader to help us change ourselves. For I felt, and I still do, that insight and understanding can help us bring our split selves into some kind of unity—and this seems to me important for every individual in our times.

Herbert Read has said, in his *Philosophy of Art*, that this age we live in needs autobiography perhaps more than all else; and yet, we have so few that are really good. Some of the best, I think, are those written by painters, and actors. At least, they tie our senses to the specifics of the world we live in and pull us away from abstractions and generalities. We need autobiographies to offset the flood of propaganda that drowns our own heartbeat; we need them because we need individuals of stature; we need them to offset the totalitarianism that is not only political but economic, and that comes not only out of the political dictator's mind but out of Madison Avenue, and from sheer aggregates. It is not easy to see individuals in a world of three billion people who inevitably become reduced to anonymous statistics and masses and programs to be stuffed into IBM machines.

Autobiography can stem this tide: it can remind men that they are individuals, each different from every other one of the three billion, and these differences are to be cherished for they are important to the future and to the self.

But must we write an autobiography because it is good for our times? The only way to answer that is to say we *cannot* write for that reason—although our times may need it. We write because of an urgent necessity to create out of our ten billion acts and thoughts and feelings a story of our life that is essentially true and meaningful. It is a great and daring creative act—this giving meaning to what might be only amorphous and absurd, were we not to seek the intense and profound awareness that transforms as it creates the story we set down. The meaningless ashes are brought to life by the phoenix of awareness.

CALL ME ISHMAEL*

The mysteries of autobiography are so deep rooted, so hidden and hard to come by, that one cannot name them easily. Perhaps a better word to use than mystery is paradox. For this is obvious: when one earnestly searches for one's real self, when one calls the word *I?* immediately six, seven, or eight voices answer: *Here!* There is a power struggle among the aspects of one's nature, as would-be selves suddenly claim a dominant role in the story. If the story concerns a matter as subjective as one's belief about the human condition the difficulties grow. For not only is there the subtle problem of whose belief, which part of the self's belief, and the cruder problem of the public self holding a hand over one's secret mouth; there is also the almost inescapable betrayal of belief by one's vocabulary. "It is almost impossible to hold a belief and to define it at the same time," Charles Williams once said. This elusiveness of belief hinges on more than a choice of metaphor, or an adverb throwing one off: it lies in the character of the multirooted belief itself which, having

* This is a fragment, headed at the top by LS, "Prologue to my book: *The Creative Uncertainty*," date uncertain, but it would seem one of the last things she wrote.

crept into bone and bloodstream and acts and values, cannot suddenly be abstracted from such a comfortably non-verbal home and placed in the cramped quarters of a book.

The novelist is wise: *Call me Ishmael,* he says—and what happens? Like magic, a real self appears: suddenly there is Ishmael, whole in time and space as one never sees one's own self. Ishmael? Ah . . . the novelist knows when Ishmael died—and this one never knows about one's self. Without that knowledge of the last chapter of one's own story, we can never quite know who we are—for that last chapter changes everything. Yes, everything: just a little. However sure we may be of "what we believe" about our universe, our hometown, our secret self, the age we live in, or God, or good and evil, or what we believe we have come to know about time or space or rocks or grace or charity or mobs or music or suffering or sex, however searching or questioning, these beliefs turn to ashes on our death— and out of the ashes rises the Phoenix, the real Self we never really found.

Yes, it is better to create an "Ishmael" if we want to come close to the truth. That prickly word: how hard it is to remember that one never *finds* truth, one creates it. This is why a novelist can sometimes create a character rich with a wisdom which the novelist has never revealed in his own life; why his character can "believe" something that seems to him unchangeable, while the selves of the novelist's own life are crazily shifting beliefs from act to act and year to year. So, even though I confess the fallibility of personal memory and self-analysis, even though I am aware of the endless minutiae of my past, and feel with the weight of tons of knowledge that I can never know that last chapter of my life—even so, I cling to the feeling that it is valid to try to get a bit of it all together, to stand back and scan my horizons, to look behind me at the strange patterns my careless and cautious footprints made through the years; to take it all and fit it somehow into a design to which I can say Yes; there is a hunger (valid or not) to call absurd what deserves that word and to call purposeful that which should be so—and probably is, "since we human beings so urgently feel the need of it."

WOMAN BORN OF MAN*

At the University of Florida last May I spoke on the mysteries of
autobiography. My title was: "[Autobiography as a] Dialogue
between King and Corpse"—between, in a sense, life reigning supreme and death. But as I worked on that speech, as I searched for
the elusive Self that the writer tries to find as he writes his autobiography, I became fascinated by a nagging fact. Why hasn't a Western
woman written a great autobiography? Couldn't one woman find her
real Self—couldn't she, somehow, plunge deeply, roam widely
enough to find the answer to Who am I? Why do women find it so
difficult to search for their identity as persons?

I had to force myself to stop those questions for they were taking
me straight to the Garden of Eden. So I turned away from the garden
and went back to my dialogue between the king and the corpse.

But ever since, I have been thinking about Eve. Ever since Eve
appeared, men have been having a hard time. So have women—but
more of that later. The Garden of Eden, Eve and Adam and the

---

* An informal speech given at Stetson University, DeLand, Florida, May 1963.

Snake of Evil can support a thousand interpretations. It is myth rooted as deeply as the human language can go. I like to think of it as the story of the birth of *homo sapiens*. A species we can name *homo* was probably here a half-million years, but men became human, sapient, only when they became aware of evil. But I think we are wrong to overstress this; for the knowledge of evil came only after man became aware of himself. To become aware of himself as Something Else, he had to split in two—in order that he might step back and look at what he saw. So, Eve was born; so, the symbol was born—and forever afterward this split in man was deep and could not be healed.

There Eve stood: man's Other Self—a different Self, yes; above all else Eve was his mirror: he could look in her eyes and see strange and awesome reflections of his own nature—and always he saw more, he saw Something Else and he was terribly frightened by what he saw, and by what he had created.

This woman whom man has created has haunted us females throughout the ages. For centuries, man has seen us as Something Dreadful and To Be Feared; and then, unable to live with this terror he has created, he turns around and makes Woman into the Pure, the Good, the All Loving, into Perfection itself. He has switched this image of woman from Madonna to Bitch, and close to both is always the Terrible Witch; in Asia, she has been the Goddess of Mercy with a thousand hands to carry out her merciful errands and she has also been the Dark Kali, the goddess who in Indian lore throws her babies into the burning pit. In Greek lore she was the Furies, the avenging maenads ready to tear the wrong-doer to pieces; ready to tear the Orphic Poet to pieces. You remember the Orpheus story: how the Furies tore Orpheus to pieces when he returned from Hell without Eurydice. They tore his flesh to pieces and threw his head into the river; and that head continued singing as it floated down toward the seas. They could not kill man's poetry; they could not stop the search for the deep truths that the poet is always after. Of all the myths that should be soothing to men—and indeed, to all the human race, including women—is this Orpheus myth. However hellish is evil it can not destroy the truth which somehow escapes the human body and lives on in the human spirit.

In our own time, in my lifetime, we have had the sacred woman of the South, and we have had Mom who dominates and domineers over her sons—and daughters—until she tears their strength from them. In the Middle Ages and on until the Renaissance men created another image of woman: the image of a woman so lovely and so capable of love that she must be worshiped by men. This image of woman, given us in an imperishable form by Dante, still lingers today. Beatrice: the girl he worshipped, the woman he adored, the lovely, ineffable creature who had a touch of holiness in her but not a holiness to be feared; one, on the contrary, to be genuflected to. This image of Beatrice, this symbol of romantic love continued to grow through the next decades; and to take a deep grip on men's imaginations. For the sake of this Lovely Woman men strove to be pure; for her sake, they wrestled with angel and devil to make of themselves something fit to be loved by her. In the Arthurian legends, this Lovely Woman grows in her power over men: we have Lancelot, struggling to be worthy of the woman he loved; we have Galahad seeking the Holy Grail, pure in heart, pure in act. And yet, in this strange and beautiful legend which had deeply affected everyone in Western culture, there are whispers, rumors, echoes of another kind of woman; there is evil lurking nearby; not even in this completely romantic period of man's relationship with woman did evil wholly disappear. It was always there; something in man's nature knew he had over-idealized woman; something whispered to him to take care, to watch out.

One cannot help but think of that dreadful scourge we call Puritanism and witch hunting as being a reaction to the beauty and purity and loveliness and worship of woman during the eleventh, twelfth, thirteenth centuries. Slowly things changed; they had to. Man was creating woman, borning her again and again to fit his dreams and his needs and his hopes, but the reality of woman always appeared, showing him a glimpse of something he had denied or never seen. After so much goodness, after so much worship, it was inevitable that man should turn on woman and burn her at the stake as a witch. Joan of Arc had to appear after so long a time of Beatrice and Iseult; the ugly nameless witches of New England had to come and haunt men's souls after they had turned from God to the worship of Woman, and from the worship of woman to the worship of a sexless body. Woman became Temptation; then she became Evil itself; and this terror of the seventeenth and eighteenth centuries dribbled over into the nineteenth century—but not for long.

A curious thing began to happen in this age of reason, this age of the overesteem of science and the scientific method. Another split took place; Man was trying to be more reasonable. He was finding it hard to believe in the madonna and the witch simultaneously; hard to fear the dread Female and to worship her purity and gentleness. Slavery helped him. The woman with a dark skin entered his life. We have never quite faced up to the significance of this encounter between white man and dark woman. Somehow much in the white woman that he could not come to terms with, the schizophrenic split he had made in her nature—the sacred madonna and the bitch he had created of her—could now be projected, in part, onto another female: under slavery, he could keep his pure white "madonna" and have his dark tempestuous "prostitute" (thereby robbing each of half her human wholeness). Echoes of this we can hear today in the overtones of demagogues' speeches as they try to arouse old fears, old temptations, old conflicts in the minds of a new generation. Back of the southern people's fear of giving up segregation is this fear of giving up the "dark woman" who has become a symbol which the men no longer wish to attach to their own white women. This is complex, abstruse, primitive stuff; we won't go into it further here, but it is part of the centuries-old segregation complex from which we all, white and dark, are suffering today.

But along with the reason and rationality of the nineteenth century—along with the encounter with the dark woman who began to be loaded with temptation and dread—came a new creature made by man. This creature was the little girl, the woman who never grew up (and therefore could never dominate a man), the doll who lived in the doll house.

It is interesting that Ibsen wrote of her first in that classic, A Doll's House, which has again acquired meaning for us in the mid-twentieth century. The Scandinavians did not have the dark woman on whom to push much of the burden of fantasy which now loaded the white woman. It was therefore easier for Ibsen to see, earlier than others, how man was once more creating woman in an image he could live with more comfortably in the scientific age. The doll; the pretty girl who never grew up in mind; the soft, warm girlish creature who obeyed her husband's wishes.

What a hard time man had during the last twenty thousand years, creating a woman he enjoyed being around. He would try one thing, then it would snowball into Something Else; he would split her, then the split part of her became a ghost that haunted his soul and his nights; he made her into a pure thing and discovered that the sort of purity he had created was icy cold and not something one's body longs to be near. He made of her sacred woman, then bitch; then witch; he worshipped her as Beatrice and abandoned her later for a dark woman's captive body; and his relationships with women became something we have not even begun to untangle today. But when he turned her into a pretty little doll he hoped it would work. And it did, for many girls. Look around you today, in the South especially, and you will still find women sixty-five and seventy years old with doll faces; with minds as soft as a marshmallow; with souls drained and emptied. Ibsen, with the prophetic insight of a poet, saw this long before others did.

But—even as he tossed the bombshell into the complacent minds of people who thought now the relationships between men and women were just fine and dandy; men could feel big and powerful as they bossed their little dolls around—here came women screaming about their need for human rights. They didn't call them human rights: they called them woman's rights; and men laughed big, and kidded their wives and daughters, trying to drown out the women's loud cries. But the women kept on; they were not non-violent as are the southern Negroes in today's movement; they were violent women; they marched with banners; they declared they had a right to wear bloomers if they wanted to; they declared they could smoke if they wanted to; they marched and made speeches and broke windows and were jailed.

Personally, I was a little embarrassed by all the furor about women voting. You see, I was rather like you: by that time, by the time I was in college, though we still couldn't vote we had acquired a great many little privileges and rights: we could wear bloomers in gym classes; we could wear divided skirts when riding horses; we did sneak a cigarette if we wanted to. We sneaked away from the chaperones, too. We felt we were doing all right; and when we read about those women in the late and middle nineteenth century screaming for woman's rights, we sometimes laughed. What my generation did not know was how many important legal rights had been won by those screams: rights that have to do with property, with the right to get divorce, with the right to hold on to one's own money, etc. We were a little ashamed of those brave but rather noisy women who won for us such a nice handful of our civil rights. Of course, we don't have all of them now; but we have a great many.

And these women did this for us. Women whose names we do not easily remember.

After the First World War we acquired the right to vote. By that time we had cut our hair—I was the first girl in my town to do so—we could wear our dresses up to our knees, we were even wearing shorts, on occasion; we were throwing our weight around in small ways; we were flaming youth.

But we never really valued what these brave women had won for us. There are young women today who do not vote; millions who do not study the problems about which we are voting. There are millions who go to college without once realizing how many women struggled through a lifetime to make it possible for girls to go to college.

But we, of my generation, did take advantage of college; we did go out into the world hungering for careers; marriage was important if we could find the right man, but we were awfully persnickety creatures and as you can see, quite a few of us did not marry, because we wanted two things: we wanted an interesting career and we wanted an interesting man to live with. It was easier to find the interesting career than the interesting man. Men wanted us to be dolls and not talk, except baby talk. But we were not talking dolls and we let our boy friends know it and they gave us one scared look and went flying down the street hoping to meet a pretty little doll who couldn't talk sense. There were still plenty of these around. And so the population explosion went on its way.

What happened to us? To those of us who wanted interesting careers and interesting men to be around? We often found both; but it was easier to find interesting men in the professions and in the business world than in the home. We had many interesting men for friends. Let it go at that . . . We were rather proud that we had sense; we could be modest but we still respected our abilities and talents; but we discovered men did not want their women to have brains; or if they had them they mustn't use them, and it hurt, it hurt like hell if I may say so, to find that the interesting men liked us in the office and laboratory and on the stage but most of them didn't want women like us in their home. So we finally had to swallow hard and admit that while we had won the battle we had lost the war.

Another generation came along; they took for granted the privileges we and the nineteenth-century woman had won for them; the positions we pioneers had opened up for them. They took for granted that they could have careers in business, in science, in the arts, in the social sciences, etc. They took the gains that women had struggled for so completely for granted that they did nothing to protect them. When men came home from the Second World War fatigued and exhausted spiritually, wanting only the home they remembered when they were kids, wanting a wife that would be like Mom, wanting children, wanting to forget this terrifying, atom bomb–ridden world we all have made for ourselves, the young women succumbed to their men's desires. They gave up their careers and went home and began to raise babies, so many babies that now everybody is worrying about a world overrun with babies.

The men who had been overseas came home fatigued, yes; but they also came home blackmailing the American girl. They talked about how feminine the Japanese girl is, how she waits on her husband, kneels before him, soothes him and makes home a haven for him; they told about how marvelous the South Seas girls were in love-making; they whispered that even the German girl—always in our minds as the hausfrau we would not be—did not dominate her husband as many American girls did, but let him dominate her.

American girls went into a panic. They began to wipe out all evidence that they had brains or education; they might have their Master's or their Ph.D. but they'd never mention it. They would try to be as genuflecting as the lovely Japanese girl, they'd try to be as delightful in love-making as those South Seas girls, they'd try to bend to their husband's wishes as did the German girl. And this was not all they had to face up to. A total misunderstanding of psychiatry and psychoanalysis had created some nasty stereotypes of the dominating Mom, the quietly domineering woman who was making her man weak and impotent; of the woman who took her frustrations out on her children, turning out a generation of sick, lost, frightened children. And all this was true—but only in part. Women were frustrated, but nobody stopped to ask who had frustrated them. Here was an educated generation of brilliant women who were told they should only raise children and run a household. Careers? A laugh could be heard everywhere: a normal woman, they said, wouldn't want a career. She must have a father complex; she feels more male than female. Then came the next whisper: maybe she *is* more male than female.

Oh it has been a mess, my dears, let me tell you. A whole generation of brilliant women brilliantly trained, with minds as keen as or keener than their husbands', forced to close all doors, forced to stop thinking, to stop creating, to stop using their talents—and what do they do instead? They clean house, for they now have no servants, they cook, they tend the kids, they chauffeur all day long; and at times they try to look sexy and act sexy because all the magazines say they must do this. They must be sexy and charming no matter how tired they are after doing the washing and the scrubbing and running the vacuum, and dashing to the Brownie meeting, and the PTA meeting, and picking up the kids from dancing class, and picking up the little sad one from psychotherapy, maybe. And television commentators and ads and magazine editors have pushed this idea of the new, highly skilled doll who mustn't use her skills.

Now where are we?

You are entering a world where women do not have quite as many rights as my generation had, and not nearly as many privileges.

I don't want to scare you, but you are entering a world where you are supposed to be a highly mechanized (and sexy) doll and nothing much else. If you decide to be a novelist, a writer—as I did—you will have to learn to put up with being called in a sneering tone a "lady novelist," you will have to put up with a resentment from men if you create male characters [who are real and vital and complex]. They will yell at you, "How could you have known?" They will look you up and down and say, "And how could you have known all this without being married?" And while it is not necessary to use many four-letter words in your books, you will find if you use one you are likely to be criticized—though male writers are not.

You will find that if you teach you are not likely to get the top jobs; if you are in a lab you are likely to be an assistant; you will find it is not much easier today for a woman to be a doctor than it was when I was a young girl. You will find it just as hard to break into a profession, to go to the top in a business, as it was when I came along. You will find that women do not receive equal pay for equal work. You will find that you have only a few more rights and privileges than did nineteenth-century women—except you may go almost anywhere. There are men's clubs you have to enter by the side door if you eat with your friend or husband in the "women's dining room"; and in politics you will have fully as hard a job getting elected as would a Negro.

This is in the United States. In parts of Asia, the women are in politics, they are fully represented in their legislative halls: here, in the United States, we women are in a definitely backward situation.

Whose fault is it? Let me say at once: it is our own. We gave up; we took the rights we had gained for granted; we fell for the feminine mystique that put women in the mid-twentieth century back in Ibsen's Doll's House.

It is our fault—nobody else's. We have taken the humiliations without talking back; we have bowed our heads and stepped off the sidewalk of careers when somebody pushed us. We have not demanded equal pay for equal work. Why? I am not sure I know. We were afraid we'd be masculine and unattractive; we were afraid we'd be called feminists as were our grandmothers; we were afraid to work for our rights for fear we would have to give up our privileges as sought-after women.

But you see, this is nothing but anxiety; it is a neurotic reaction to stress that is wholly unnecessary. Women are quite capable of marrying well and with love, raising a few children, and still holding down interesting jobs. If they can't do it all simultaneously, they can do it in sequence. They can build up their careers until they are in their late twenties, then marry; they can keep house, be marvelous wives, and raise a few children; then they can return into the world and pick up careers; they will find their marriage has been a good thing; they will find they have grown in wisdom and shrewdness, too; and they will make better careers than ever.

They will also find that men today are not as afraid of their own lack of brains as they used to be; men have proved their worth and their intelligence, in science at least; maybe not yet have they proved that they have much wisdom in world political affairs; but they can stand side by side without feeling inferior. They had to get used to our having brains, you know; the sight of us showing our talents and brilliance alarmed them, at first. But they are used to us, now; just as we are beginning to get used to having free, unsegregated, bright, clever Negroes around.

It all comes down to our mutual willingness to become human: to think of ourselves first as human beings and second as women and men, and third as being different in appearance and talents and abilities and insights.

The role of human beings in a world environment is going to be your role. You will not find it easy to measure up; you may even have to give up a few of your privileges in order to enjoy your human rights—but it may be well worth it.

I am not one of the people who view the future with anxiety. I know we can blow ourselves off the face of the earth; but if women will speak out more, do more, work more, create more, I don't think it will happen: for women are close to life, they hold it within their own bodies, they live with it when it is young; and this experience gives them a special responsibility to do all in their power to keep us from nuclear war, to protect the lives and future of all the earth's children. And it is here in human relations, in protecting life in its rich variety, that women can show their real strength and use their brains.

But remember: let your men dream; let them keep borning women they can endure—give them this privilege, and you can get and keep your full human rights. But maybe you will have to remind them now and then that what they dream up, their images, are symbols, not women. After all, men don't really want to live with Lolita; they couldn't endure it. They do need to keep their symbols in poetry and art. Then and only then can they live with you real women and enjoy it. . . .

EXTRACTS FROM THREE LETTERS

I*

My thinking is of a different mode [from that of Dave in *One Hour*]; I am a suffering human being who sees the world through her suffering; who has learned most of what she knows not from books but her own existence. I am the opposite of easy-going; where Dave had always thought he had made mistakes, had erred but had never really sinned, I from the time I was five years old was making the lives of my elders miserable with my searching, repetitive question: "What is the unpardonable sin? What is it?" And my other questions: "What was the beginning—and when is the end? when? when? . . ."

My childhood was filled with the thought of time, my time, their time, everybody's time, God's time . . . I felt it circling, I could not see it as a straight line stretching from the six days of creation to Judgment Day and on and on. I remember the curious sense of the future I had: always a magic door: in the future these questions could be

* From a letter to Rollo May, dated December 26, 1959.

transcended; in the future I would become different from what I then was; in the future—the future held everything for me: by "everything" I mean the explanation of everything. I asked the existential questions without access to the existential vocabulary.

Well—I did not mean to write my autobiography for you; but I am temperamentally so different from Dave that I found myself stunned when the reviewers felt that I was using him as my mouthpiece. No character in the book was my mouthpiece; the closest would be Jane, I think; yet I am not Jane at all; for Jane had ceased aching and paining as I always have, and am afraid always will.

There is a piece of me in all these characters, of course; I am a little like Grace, yes; I am enough like Dave to love him and know him, his mode of thinking, his way of feeling; I am also enough like Mark to feel very close to him. But I think a novelist puts not only herself, aspects of herself, in her novel; she puts the aspects of all the people she loves or hates and, therefore, *becomes*. The novel is full of my loves and hates, of course; and how could I have written Renie, had I not felt what Renie felt! Characters, I think, come out of every phase of our own being, our own growth as a person; but they also come out of the people who have been loved or hated by the author; and also out of the people over whom one has suffered, and about whom one has thought the whole night through. And then, one picks up vivid pieces of people without knowing it: as one walks the street, goes into small town stores—or the big city stores (for I talk with everyone I meet or I listen or sometimes just look). An author, an artist, is like something magnetic: a magnetized piece of metal that picks up things without intending to. And, of course, I have always been the kind of person whom people confess to. Sometimes, in a store, suddenly the clerk will pour out her deepest anxieties or her bitterest perplexities; the children always did in my camp; so did the counselors; so did people in my hometown—businessmen who have not talked, really communicated, even with their wives, will suddenly begin to talk about the most profoundly felt questions they have asked themselves. And this, in a sense, gives a person quite a wealth of material, writhing, live material, ever-changing material.

There is no act of the human being that seems to me more complex than that of one who writes a novel, if it is written with all doors open and an escalator that goes vertically from the depths to the heights. When this state of mind comes, one lives in a new, a totally different way: one does not feel barriers between one and the characters one has created (at least there are moments when one does not—at other times, the characters will suddenly close up, or withdraw, or retreat in a baffling silence, a terrible blankness).

The most devastating feeling I have, after each book (I had it after *Strange Fruit*, after *Killers of the Dream*, after *The Journey*, and after *One Hour*) is this: I feel, about two weeks after I've written the last line, when it is all finished, that now and only now am I ready to write that book; now, I tell myself, I have learned enough from my own characters and scenes to really write the book I intended to write. That is a sick sort of feeling. I suppose the only cure is to write another; but then I shall explore so many new places, learn so much about the new characters as I create them, that at the end I shall feel I am only then "ready" to write it.

II*

A curious thing about *Strange Fruit* is that it proved, for me, to be therapy that removed a long amnesia about my hometown. I was born and reared in "Maxwell, Georgia." At the age of seventeen I left there. The night I was graduated from high school, I came back from the auditorium, changed from my white accordion-pleated dress, put on a coatsuit and came to Clayton, our new home which for a few years had been our summer home. I left that wonderful sixteen-room house in which I was born, set in the middle of a town block, surrounded with great live oaks heavy with moss; I hardly looked back at it that night. I got on the train—and slowly, creepingly, I began to forget the town in which I was born.

You see, my father had lost all his business (naval stores and shipping, then being affected by World War I complexities) and our

* From a letter to Maxwell Geismar, dated January 1, 1961.

home; I heard him criticized for the first time in my life. We were going to be poor (and I had never been poor); we were going to have a rather bleak life for a while, and I knew it. All I wanted was never to let Mother and Dad know I cared. So nature helped me out a bit.

Hard years followed. I worked my way at college and at the [Peabody] Conservatory in Baltimore (by accompanying voice students, dancers, etc.). I went to China. Prior to this, I had had a love affair, some strands of which perhaps entered into the Tracy-Nonnie relationship—though the man was a Viennese violinist; yet there were dreadful psychological and cultural barriers between us, and I could not break them. So then, ten years later, on a trip to Florida, I went back to that little town.

When I arrived, I was a complete stranger; I could not find my way even to my old home; when someone gave me directions I drove there, stopped the car in front of the big lawn (which looked rather small after living, as I do now, on a big mountain). But it wasn't home; I sat there trembling, for I could not feel that this was home. I went out to the old graveyard, groped my way down a street I had walked hundreds of times in my childhood but it was strange to me now and I stopped twice to ask directions to a graveyard that I once knew as well as my own name. I saw my grandfather's grave there and that of my favorite brother who had died at college; but it all seemed strange and remote.

Ten years later, I began to write *Strange Fruit*. I worked on it six years and when I completed it my memory of ten thousand, maybe ten million details, had returned. I drove through it again, after the book was published (with dark glasses on, not knowing how the people would feel about me). All of it was like it had been when I left there at age seventeen—although it had actually changed quite a bit, especially during those last ten years. I knew my way around perfectly. The town had come back to me, always now to live with me. The story, the plot, the four or five main characters of S.F. had little to do with my hometown. They were created by me; but some minor characters I am afraid I sketched, unknowing that I did so in many cases, from real people. At any rate, many former citizens of that town have told my brothers that they were gasping with shock and delight as they read the book; and that they could hardly believe that I, at seventeen, knew these people so well.

So—when I was told that I had written a "problem novel" I was bemused; yes, I had—but it was my own problems, my profound, existential problems that I had written about. Yet I was not naive; after working on the book for four years, I told Paula Snelling, "If I don't watch out, people are going to think I am writing about race relations." I had for a long time thought of white and black people as just people; I, myself, grew more aware of the paradoxes, the ambiguities of our black-white life as I was writing. I shocked myself, at times, with my sudden, quick intuitions. I wrote down things I did not know were true until I saw them staring back at me on the page. It was actually a double journey for me: back into my earliest childhood, recovering what I had left there; into the present, seeing what we bewildered, blind human beings had done to ourselves and to others and to our future. There were moments of sudden vision, when I saw as Saul of Tarsus must have, what segregation as symbol and symptom actually was; and I wrote with immense passion at the times I felt this sudden insight. But the passion did not have to do entirely with Negroes and whites, and the South with its abysses and its rickety swinging half-visible bridges; it had to do also with my own personal and not racial experiences. In a sense, I think I used race as a symbol of the splits, the estrangements in my own life. How curious we are! When we are creating, we not only follow the bird's way making a nest out of whatever is closest to us, making it to fit a form we (like the bird) have in our bloodstream; we do more, sometimes; we follow the Chinese bird's way, that strange little bird that regurgitates what it has eaten and then makes its nest of this translucent jelly. A delicacy to human palates.

III*

In *Strange Fruit* I was writing about my past and yours and every Westerner's, exploring the crooked trails that lead to hell, peering

* Recipient and date of this letter are uncertain.

into the dark jungle of lost minds. To me, what was important was to create a town, area by area by area then level by level by level, until I had secured it in its depths and its heights. I chose a southern town because I was born in one and knew it in my bones and blood; but I also chose it as a symbol of man's brokenness in this modern world, man's deep split, man's alienation from himself and his God. I chose it, too, because I felt that in this small space I could catch both God and the Devil, that I could hold for a little while both good and evil. My symbols appeared to me as I went along; I did not consciously tell myself that Alma (the mother) was Southern Tradition until I had half written the book; I did not tell myself that Tracy, the young southern man, was a symbol of the South's moral weakness, its ambivalences and ambiguities, its fixation on the past (Alma), until I hit a certain chapter and then it blazed out at me. I did not tell myself that Maxwell, Georgia, was the West and all the white people in it until I had almost finished the book. I knew it was the United States; the white race everywhere: that dawned on me more slowly. There was one thing my little town did not have (and this may be why it is liked so much in Asia) and that was science. Neither gadgets nor scientific method had invaded my little town of the 1920s. But this seemed right to me, too, for actually wherever the two races live together there is a curious attachment to the before-science era. Even where there are giant machines, etc., the minds are still pre-scientific. And there is a layer of this in every man.

I suppose it was inevitable that my book be picked up and read as a book written by a woman with a cause. I am not ashamed of causes: as a human being, I feel deeply concerned and cannot shake off my responsibility to do something. As a writer, I still feel it, but I write to explore the unknown, to answer my questions or else find new questions. One little book I wrote with the conscious purpose of helping about race relations: *Now Is the Time*. I read it again after five years (a few days ago) and found it good. I was amazed at its simplicity, its good sense, even its wisdom. (You see I have to say these things even out loud, occasionally, to keep from blowing my brains out in my discouragement at the critics' and reviewers' refusal to accept me as a writer.) I have been curiously smothered during the past nine years;

indeed, ever since *Killers of the Dream*. When writers about "race" are discussed, I am never mentioned; when southern writers are discussed, I am never mentioned; when women writers are mentioned, I am not among them; when best-sellers are discussed, *Strange Fruit* (which broke every record for a serious book) is never mentioned. This is a curious amnesia; I have smiled at it, have laughed at it; but I know what it has done to me in sales and in prestige.

This is frank talk. Do not, I beg you, be embarrassed by it. I can still laugh it off most of the time; but now and then, I truly wonder. Whom, among the mighty, have I so greatly offended!